Forever Sober

Forever Sober

By

Douglas H. Ruben, Ph.D.

PRINTING HISTORY
First Printing 2000

PRINTED IN THE UNITED STATES OF AMERICA.
10 9 8 7 6 5 4 3 2 1

1st Books-rev. 2/21/00

About The Book

Stop Drinking TODAY!

Addictions specialist, Dr. Douglas Ruben has done it again! His latest book explodes the myths of alcoholism for what it is: A power-hungry craving programmed in childhood. FOREVER SOBER graphically reveals secrets of rapid nondrinking and lasting sobriety. Explicitly told is why addicts drink, why sobriety fails, and what to do about it. And that' not all.

Dr. Ruben prescribes rapid cures for social drinkers turned addicts. Easy-to-use steps convert heavy drinkers into nondrinkers; cravings vanish and healthy habits flourish. His life-engineering tools propel recovery to new heights. Plus, families get armed with ammunition dealing with sobriety.

"An indispensable bible using scientific methods for everyday problems."

ASK HIM--What drives alcoholics to abuse? How does it consume their lives? Is changing addiction like flicking a light switch? And when is recovery *really effective?*

CONTENTS

Author's Note

Okay, so what's your story? Everybody has a story. Go ahead, admit it. I'll tell you a secret if you tell me a secret. It's truth-or-dare time. So, spill the beans. Let it out. Show me how anatomy you really have.

Something, somewhere happened to you in your life causing irrepressible memories. I know. I've been there. And, yes, I have a story.

I won't regal you with a litany of childhood nightmares or even the boo-hoos of my adult life. That's not where the story begins. It begins with drinking. But I wasn't the drinker. I was the one who helped the drinker.

Did you ever do that? Help a drinker? Isn't that a bitch? The trouble with caring is that you really get into people you care about. I found myself deeply entrenched with alcoholics and passionately identifying with their plight more intimately than I feel today toward my family. Weird? Maybe. But caring is a special gift. Do it a little and you feel guilty for being greedy and not giving another person you're all. Do it too much and you soak up another person's absurd and sordid life, wondering how you got there in the first place, and helpless to pull out.

That's about where I was. Somewhere in between over-caring with my head sunken into the toilet of patient's raw sewage, and feeling overwhelmed by aimlessly misguided on how to cure them.

About 18 years ago I was in the odd position of living at home after spending almost 4 years away at college. Some fun. It took some adjusting to, I can assure you. But my parents were sympathetic to my financial woes and thought they'd stick it out with me while I impatiently waited for acceptance into a doctoral program.

I was home, all right, and inspired by my zeal to save the world. I guess all neophyte psychologists have this complex. The Hercules complex of feeling you can conquer and treat any problem; no personality disorder is insurmountable. It's a good philosophy for beginners. Remove and replace, and turn misery into happiness. Dig in like a surgeon removing a bullet and repair the mind and body so that it functions at full speed again.

Sure, I'd like to do that. But when you are hungry for miracles, high expectations are your cup of tea. You breathe it; believe it, and act as if you are God's messenger. Any openings for St. Peter? I thought there was.

So, eager-beaver that I was, I landed a job at a private psychiatric hospital working in the social work department. I was a "clinical aide," a euphemism for glorified nurse with no RN background and not enough psychology background to merit being called a therapist. Stuck in professional purgatory, clinical aides fit in where they could. In group therapy, I made sure patients attended and contributed input. For individual therapy, I was a lifeguard saving patients from drowning in their emotional tears after ravaged by unsympathetic psychiatrists who informed the patients they were crazy and weren't ready for discharge. I defused the patients charged emotions and let them know everything was all right.

I'd say, "Don't worry,"

"Why? Why shouldn't I worry? You get to go home tonight whereas I have to stay here."

And the patient was right. I never knew how to answer them. Was I really relieving their hurt?

I think so.

After a month of baby-sitting the real clinical staff, I was given the dubious honor of switching to midnight shift on the alcohol rehabilitation unit. That meant working from 9 PM to 8 AM in the morning. And let me tell you, for all of you hard-working factory and hospital workers slaving the graveyard shift, my heart goes out to you. I don't know how you do it. I still don't know how I did it. By 2:00 AM, my eyes were shut. We're not talking eyelid flutter or lapsing periodically into semi-sleep. Try ironclad locked. My eyes closed like a 700-pound bag of sand. I was asleep. I was gone. And the only way I kept awake either was to watch educational movies or arrange my break for a brief naptime.

Breaks were scarce, so I opted for the educational movies.

With the reels grinding on the old projectors, I impersonated

Siskel and Ebert. I became my own movie critic. I watched at least twenty dramatizations of alcoholics ruining their family and saw graphically vivid types of damage to the human body from overdrinking; cirrhosis of the liver, respiratory and circulatory failure, diabetes, endocrine failure, brain cell destruction, and bloody, fatal vehicular accidents. It felt like I'd being riding a roller coaster through Gray's Anatomy. Bones, skin, muscle, organs--everything that can contaminate, destroy, and ultimately kill the living body was visually panoramic and kept my eyelids open. I imagined being the villain in *A Clockwork Orange* having my eyelids clipped open while forced to visually ingest painfully shocking and inhumane scenarios.

I got the gist of the alcoholic's doomsday world and decided not to watch reruns of the movies when other patients watched them. While I got enlightened by the movies and, yes, even remembered what I saw, the movies were only a steppingstone to my real experience with drinkers.

Nothing was more powerful than what happened to me one early morning near the end of my shift. With my last break taken, I kept thinking about how good sleep would feel after I got off work. I think I even dozed off while quietly sitting at the nurse's station. There was nothing to do, nobody to talk to, and I was struggling with empty boredom. I'd drift off for a second or two and awake with a jerking motion, hoping nobody saw me. Thank God they didn't.

Then it happened. I received an emergency call from the admissions unit alerting me to the arrival of an ETHANOL patient in withdrawal. ETHANOL? What was that? I knew from staff meeting and sneaking a peak at charts which patients were alcoholics and who had other emotional problems. You could test me on any patients--I'd proudly show you who had what diagnosis. I had an eye for sizing up the patients. I could spot schizophrenics. I cold give you a tour of anxiety patients. And Organics? I was a pro at finding them. But ETHANOL? I had no clue whom they were and what they did.

That's when Patient X arrived like lightening speed onto the unit accompanied by two nurse's aides and a psychiatrist. I sat motionless and watched this ordeal like a spectator seated in the upper-deck bleachers looking down on a sportsfield. Like a bystander, I watched in amazement and couldn't believe my eyes. Patient X was staggering as he clumsly made his way to the nurse's desk in my direction. His eyes turned upward in his sockets revealing he whites of his pupils. His mouth dropped open with saliva dripping out of it. His shirt was covered with vomit from his neck down to his waist. The rank odor reached my nostrils in record time and took me aback. "Gross" wasn't even the word for it. Try suffocating.

I watched his body jerk like an epileptic seizure as he nearly fell down; nursing aides rushed to grab him before he tumbled and they tried seating him in a wheelchair. He didn't cooperate. His spastic kicking of arms and legs knocked one aide against the wall. The other aide steadied his position. Then he leaped back into Patient's X's space and grabbed Patient X's arms down while bending him at the waist to sit in the wheelchair.

Patient X wasn't about to comply. He ranted and raved at the top of his lungs using colorful four-letter words. With his profanity came a lava flow of vomit. It projected out of his mouth like a volcanic eruption spewing pieces of every meal he had in the last day.

His violent surge of vomit propelled out of his mouth and over the counter of the nurse's station, spilling on top of books, papers and yours truly. Yes, I was blessed with tomato soup and a half-cheese sandwich splattered on my shirt and dripping down my pants.

I was not a happy camper.

Patient X kept regurgitating in stereo for the next 10 minutes until his acid-tank ran out of juice. He was rushed by wheelchair into the examining room and there his loud aching noises finally subsided. His withdrawal turmoil had taken a reprieve.

Whereas, my experience with withdrawal had just begun.

Odor aside, his uncontrollable up-chucking and completely monster-like hysteria left me wide awake and ready to do a double shift. I'd never before witnessed a human being in such distress. His entire body was on fire, ravaging through his insides with a blaze of terror he couldn't stop. He was conscious but not conscientious of the devastating trauma his body suffered to fight off ETHANOL effects.

Oh, so by the way, what was ETHANOL withdrawal?

Ethanol, I learned later that evening was the psych unit term for "Alcohol." Patient X had a physical addiction to alcohol where he drank 10 to twenty beers and straight whisky every day. One day he got sick to his stomach, probably from a flu, and didn't drink as usual. Two hours past his normal drinking time his body went into convulsions and 911 was called.

Patient X exhibited the classic signs of alcohol withdrawal syndrome that occurs when excessive drinking stops for one reason or another. Your body craves the alcohol like a junkie obsessed with getting his or her next fix. Desperately the body searches the system for ETHANOL to quench its thirst. When it finds it, temporarily the body is okay and withdrawal is averted. When the body comes up empty, the body has a temper tantrum. It nose-dives into a downward spiral heading straight for body-hell. The muscles contract, glands go on a secretion binge, and internally your body is a radiator melting its insides with no coolant dousing the fire.

I stood dumbfounded opposite Patient X after he projected vomit onto my shirt. My mind spun in a hundred directions. I tried to be clinical and managed to tell the aides to "kindly get this vomiting man out of here." But really, those were just defensive words. Inside I wasn't defensive. I was nervous. I saw a human being devoured by painful torture as the result of many years of killing his body. He was suicidal-but not in the traditional use of the word. His suicide was long, drawn-out and excruciating. Hostage to his own addictive habits, Patient X had disintegrated his mind and body from first drinking in adolescence and really accelerating his intake as an adult. It didn't matter why he did it. Not then, at least. All I knew was what I saw: a UFO. No, not an unidentified flying object. Rather, an *Uncaring and Failing Organism*.

Patient X left a lasting impression on my mind. I never drank much before witnessing his withdrawal syndrome but I tied one on like most curious kids. Did I get drunk? Sure, once, maybe twice. The ultimate thrill of an out-of-the-body like experience when you feel loose, dizzy, and in sensory limbo was hard to pass up. But not any more. One eye-full of Patient's X propelling pieces of vomit and I converted to a nondrinker in seconds.

I didn't like seeing this patient in withdrawal. And today in clinical practice I work feverishly to prevent many patients from digressing to such physical collapse where their bodies are erupting and they are inescapably sucked into a withdrawal holocaust.

Not everybody of course is Patient X. Even Patient X wasn't Patient X at one time in his life. But he became an excessive drinker progressively over time as his lifestyle needs changed and his habits conveniently adapted to more than one liquor beverage. Patient X wanted more than one drink for many reasons; he gave in to his urge and had more than one drink. Twenty beers later and feeling inebriated, Patient X still wanted a drink. Was this a death wish?

No, not a death wish. More of a firing squad. Each time he imbibed in drinking binges and got lost in la-la land, he was lining up the squadron to take aim and fire at his decomposing body. Patient X gave up on being a nondrinker. He waited until that near-fatal day when a simple flu-bug nearly cost him his life and left him physically paralyzed in a pool of vomit.

Did Patient X learn from his trauma? I'd like to say there is a happy ending to the story. But, frankly, I don't really know what happened to him. What I know is what happened to me. I re-live this episode over and over in my mind every time I treat alcohol and drug abusers in outpatient and inpatient settings. I look at them squarely in the eyes as if posing a dare to them: "Are you going to vomit on me? Are you Patient X?"

Patient X is in every patient I see with a substance abuse problem. I see their drinking as absurd and vaguely demeaning to their lives. I regard their self-indulgence as a last resort to run away from life-shattering miseries they don't know how to deal with or are afraid to confront.

Yes, Patient X has made me think twice about drinking myself. I don't do it. No, I'm not a Teetotaler. I not a radical who waves poster boards of Patient X saying, "Down with drinking." I don't need to. My patients know where I come from when I announce why I want them to stop drinking.

I don't care why or how your drinking started; I'll find that out and work through it with you. But you have to do one thing for me. There are many reasons why you think you drink and why you think other people drink. . Do me a favor. Check all of these preconceptions at the door. Open the pages of this book with a pad of paper and a pencil and be prepared to write down reasons for drinking and ways to quit drinking that you've never seen before.

If you believe in Alcoholics Anonymous and that's your only way to salvation, you may be doing something right. But don't count on Alcoholics Anonymous to pull your weight in this incredibly delicate and difficult process of being what you don't want to be: a nondrinker.

This book is your blueprint for being a nondrinker. A nondrinker is not a drinker who elects not to drink. That's an alcoholic who drinks tomorrow instead of today. A nondrinker is a person who is firmly willing to be a new person in the world where everything you do does not revolve around ETHANOL. You don't think like a drinker because your thoughts lose a drinking mentality. Can you do it? Can you really defy your internal desire for alcohol?

I know you can. Because, frankly, one Patient X was enough for a lifetime.

Chapter 1

Start Your New Life Today

Are you a statistic? It's easy to become one. Ten million adults and estimates of over 3 million young people under age 18 are alcoholics. That's right, "Alcoholics." The word itself is a funny way to describe overusing a substance regarded as normal in many parts of the world. In Europe, for example, wine is like water; adults and children alike consume it with meals and for refreshment. In America, wine, beer and mixed-liquor habits are less cultural and more a social fad. You drink because it seems normal. You either grew up seeing your parents or relatives drink it. You drink because high school or college friends drank and now your habits carried on into your family life. Or, you drink because drinking does for you what a pill can do; it relieves something you don't want to feel.

Whatever the reason, drinking alcohol is only a problem when you begin to observe unusual warning signs in your life. Or, if you don't catch them-beware that others will. In this chapter you'll discover exactly when too much drinking is really too much and why lingering habits are just an excuse for not changing. But here's what you shouldn't expect from this chapter or book:

You won't be reincarnated.
You won't get a quick-fix and feel fine.
You won't be vindicated from feeling guilty.
You won't convert to a religion.

Sorry, I don't do conversions. But you might. You might undergo such a strong transformation in thinking like a nondrinker that you won't notice yourself. You may feel like you had emotional reconstructive surgery. And, assuredly, the new you may be better, not worse. You won't be transformed into some personality you think is weak, boring, and idiotic.

1

I don't turn people into idiots. I help them turn into competent, productive survivors of habits. And you're about to embark on the road to becoming this person.

And I want you to preserve your personality every step along the way of becoming a nondrinker. So, let's get started by sampling a taste of red-light-signals of drinking. You alone can figure out if you're on the one-way treadmill of drinking for the sake of drinking.

Why Yesterday is Gone

Alcohol is among the most common addictions in the world. You're not surprised, are you? Research overwhelmingly argues that early drinkers and users of mind-altering drugs are nuclear missiles headed for disaster. By adult age, casual drinkers turn heavy drinkers and are comfortable ingesting large quantities during the morning, day and night. That's a lot of drinking. Does that describe your drinking habits?

Can you fathom that? Morning, noon and night? Make a comparison to any other liquid or solid you regularly consume to get an idea of this quantity. Like, for example, lemonade. Can you imagine drinking several glasses of lemonade throughout the day? How about chewing one to two packs of gum from morning until midnight? Any food or substance taken in excess seems a bit compulsive, doesn't it? If you're not sure how preposterous this sounds, think of it this way: imagine taking 10 to twenty showers a day. Now, assuming you were not in a diseased-controlled environment requiring constant bathing, do you think you could undress, shower, and re-dress that many times in a day?

Probably not. Doing anything in large amounts requires two things:

First, you are either totally unaware of what you're doing and easily distracted. Or, second, you are methodically aware, calibrated and careful to repeat your habit multiple times a day. Extremes in either direction are the norm. Exceptions are possible but rare. For drinking, either extreme applies as well. Inattentive drinkers and habits are *Drifters*. Drifters go through life oblivious to their actions and are impulsive, disorganized and procrastinate on everything. Promises they make are shallow and unfulfilled. Drifters may drink two beers in early afternoon and seven beers in early evening without any connection between drinking episodes.

They don't "connect," since time elapse is relative. They live hedonistically for the moment and are forgetful of what they did earlier. Spontaneous, energetic and lively, Drifters seek a thrill-seeking, endorphin-pumping climax stimulated by high arousing pleasures. They are not content with a cocktail or with drinking alone. They drink for the euphoric effect in mixed company and thrive on the uninhibited person they become.

Their alter egos are *Calibrators.* Smart, savvy and methodical, Calibrators are human engineers. They know exactly what they are doing and how much alcohol will produce a desired effect. Daytime and nighttime drinking is not coincidental. Calibrators calculate their anticipated arousal down to a science. They can predict, control, and expect to get blasted on the dot. Although premeditated and decisive, Calibrators are shy. They are not barflies or socialites yuk-yuking it up around friends and strangers. Nor are they spontaneous.

Calibrators are precise They choose the time, place, and people around whom maximal drinking effect is achievable. Perfecting alcohol intake is not an art; it's an act of survival. They've learned to survive alcohol dependency by pretending they are still in control. That way, no matter how drunk they get, Calibrators can lie to themselves that they know what they are doing.

Let's review these types again:

A Drifter is a drinker who is unaware of how much he or she drinks. The person drinks spontaneously and for thrill-seeking pleasure. They don't know they are heavy drinkers are don't care about being in control.

A Calibrator is a drinker who is decisively aware of how much he or she drinks. The person drinks intentionally, methodically, and does so purely to relieve a psychological or physical condition. They know they are heavy drinkers but think they are in control since drinking is intentional.

Are you a Drifter or Calibrator? The best way to figure this one out is to ask yourself the following questions. Be honest-- real honest. Open your heart of truth as you answer the questions with a YES or NO.

1. Do you drink to relieve pain?
2. Do you drink to feel more energetic?
3. Do you drink to put you in a good mood?
4. Do you drink to make you less afraid?
5. Do you drink to get rid of boredom?
6. Do you drink to be more creative?
7. Do you drink for better sex?
8. Do you drink because you're angry?
9. Do you drink because you're depressed?
10. Do you drink so you won't feel lonely?
11. Do you drink to improve your mind?
12. Do you drink to relax yourself?
13. Do you drink alone?
14. Do you drink to build up your self-confidence?
15. Do you regularly drink to help you sleep?
16. Do you drink to avoid going to the doctor?

A YES to more than 50% of these answers means you are a Calibrator. Congratulations. You may drink spontaneously and possibly overlap some with Drifters, but your habits are mostly preconceived. You're no dummy; you know why you drink and how much of the alcohol will perfectly release the inner you.

Now, what about Drifters? Here is what most drifters answer as YES. Read through the list to see how you score:

1. Do you lose time from work due to your drinking?
2. Do you drink to feel social and get along with people?
3. Do you forget what you drink, ate, or did earlier in the day?
4. Do you crave a drink at different times of the day?
5. Do you feel you deserve a drink for anything good you do?

6. Did you ever have a complete loss of memory as a result of your drinking?
7. Have you ever done something while drinking you later regretted?
8. Do you hear others say you are a different when you drink?
9. Do you like to drink around other people?
10. Do you dare yourself to drink more each time or to drink different alcohol beverages?
11. Do you find it difficult to pull yourself away from gambling at casinos or horse-races?
12. Do you get hyped quickly and worry about the consequences of your action later?
13. Do you say things you don't mean and assume people know what you're talking about?
14. Do you love being the center of a attention?

Scores over 50% rank you a big-time Drifter. You share the very same love for excitement as Drifters do; you'd scuba dive near sharks; you'd drink until your blitzed and thrive on every second of every moment during your high. You'd chug a 12-pack down like it's water because you know there is more beer where that came from and it's all at your fingertips. Wound up and ready to spin, you constantly feel an insatiable craving to experience life to its fullest. That means climbing the highest peak, wind-surfing, bungie-chord jumping, or hypnotically drugging yourself with God-knows what chemicals until you capture that moment of Karma.

And once you get to that land of OZ, it's serenity times ten. Pure and calming bliss where you can free all of your worries and relax in the bubble-bath fantasy of your mind.

Mistakes are Okay

So, now you know who you are. Calibrators and Drifters international, unite! You've gone the gamut of hiding, pretending, and lying. Sure, intuitively you know that excessive drinking is bad for you. But like anything you do, why change a habit when that habit is helping you cope? Obviously, you won't. It's too difficult to do that. Alcohol is serving a purpose for you and you want to keep it that way.

That is because alcohol is a band-aid cure. It sedates or energizes; one or the other. Alcohol sedates by depressing the nervous system, calming down your body, and slowing down thinking. Obsessively anxious people may drink alcohol to replace tranquilizers. Highly stressed workaholics may drink alcohol to offset headaches and decompress after work. One glass of wine or beer may lower their heart rate, relax their muscles, and stop disturbing ruminations.

Alcohol, the energizer, does the opposite effect of sedation. It acts like a stimulant to feel alert, electrical and vibrant. Energizing charges you up like a runaway locomotive with unlimited strength and uninhibited fears. You can talk the talk, say what's on your mind, and take a giant leap into the social spotlight by feeling voltage rush through your body. You are a buzzing bee, fluttering around vivaciously and defying the laws of body fatigue. Depressed people who find they get stuck in low gear, for example, may find alcohol a back-up battery recharging their strength and eliminating feelings of helplessness. Chronically fatigued or pain sufferers use alcohol to block debilitating symptoms and rebound from depths of feeling immobilized. Even bored and homebound dads and moms caught in the parent trap without a ray of sunshine in their lives drink for a superficial boost.

Drinking for either reason is potentially hazardous. Calibrators and Drifters, whether drinking for energy or sedation, may enjoy too much of a good thing. Take John Schubeck, the controversial Los Angeles TV anchor who recently died. Schubeck's career was a celebrity story gone tragic with his multiple marriages, alcoholism, and bizarre sense of humor. He'd embellish crime reports and defied network censors by laughing as he cashed in his unprecedented million-dollar salary. But his career and social life plummeted when stories of his unethical escapades overshadowed his brilliant newsreporting. His life was barely held up by a thread of impulsive highs, chaotically strung together by producers who made him look better than he was.

Schubeck's life was a testimony of how Drifter's who use alcohol for energy are in big trouble. You might say actor Robert Downey Jr. is living proof of the same thing. Downy recently violated court-ordered probation by being caught inebriated. His burning desire to feel endorphins enlivened has detoured his ambition of having steady acting jobs. He, like yourself, may feel that temporary elevated body sensations are well worth the personal or financial sacrifices made when you choose alcohol over nonalcohol.

And, of course, who can forget how impulsive drinking contributed to famed princess Diana's fatal car accident. Or tragically ended a brilliant career for a Red Wing hockey player shortly after the team won the Stanley Cup Championship. Both were innocent victims of inebriated drivers whose reckless drinking habits interfered with responsible behavior.

All of these reputed drunks faced emotional downsizing. They lost respect, jobs, and suffered physical repercussions from overdoing a good thing. In the case of Princess Di's and Dodi Fayed's death, the drinking chauffeur died as well. Will that be your fate? Do you know when your drinking habits really are out of control?

I hate to be the one who blows the whistle, but you're probably guilty of many common warning signs of drinking that becomes a problem

Problem drinking occurs when you can say YES to the following:

1. I drink some amount of alcohol every day.
2. I drink in front of my friends and family and am not secretive.
3. If I am secretive, I don't care if they catch me drinking.
4. I drink little or not at all during the week but I drink heavy on weekends.
5. I have drunk to the point of blacking-out where I don't remember anything.

6. I get violent when I drink.
7. I get very quiet and withdrawn when I drink.
8. I can go hours without eating if I drink.
9. I find I can't concentrate on anything unless I drink.

YES answers are okay. Don't fight the obvious voice in your mind admitting you may have a serious drinking problem. Go ahead: confess it. Nobody cares if you confess; there's no priest here. Nobody will judge you except yourself. You are your own judge and jury. What you tell yourself stays confidentially with yourself. And, of course, what you lie to yourself stays a lie in your mind.

Look Ahead Two Steps at a Time

Breaking loose from the strongholds of habits is no easy chore. Aficionados of alcohol recovery research are boldly skeptical about what you have to do: Quit. Be totally dry and sober. Sure, you can say you'll quit and really believe your words. But terminating habits is like terminating friendships. It doesn't happen overnight.

The problems is not with you; the problem is with alcohol. Alcohol has been around a long time. For thousands of years, it has been easily available, the cheapest tranquilizer, and the simplest social entertainment. Many people still believe that alcohol has medicinal effects since it was the prime anesthetic used during pre-industrial wars such as the American Revolution and Civil War. Prevalence of alcohol almost tempts you to think it will not go away and so using less of it probably feels redeeming.

As a backlash from the drug scares of years ago, millions of parents and spouses say, "Thank goodness my child isn't on drugs," as the police drag them home drunk. Naturally they are relieved the addiction is alcohol, thinking that alcohol is culturally widespread and tolerable. Truth is, folks, alcohol really is not a good substitute for drugs. It is the most dangerous drug in our society.

And then, another school of thought prevails. It derives out of the Sobell's research a decade ago and held that moderation of drinking is better than regular daily drinking. Social or "controlled" drinking gained popularity for its liberally permissive attitude of tolerating binge drinkers since alcoholics still went to work sober and met their family responsibilities. Forgetting for the moment all of the pitfalls of this research, there is a huge problem with controlled drinking: You may feel it exonerates you from feeling guilty and responsible for overdrinking.

Plus, it's wishful thinking. It's daydreaming. Drinking in moderation actually invites greater consumption resulting in more problems and less personal control.

And, of course, happy drinkers resistant to change their habits may take another popular perspective. They may blame their drinking on inherited genes. Sure, why not? Blame your body rather than yourself. Dennis did. Dennis was a twenty-a-day beer drinker who failed miserably at quick-cures such as antabuse or inpatient hospitalizations. His high rate of recidivism, he felt, was an indication of transmittable genes from his father, also a heavy beer drinker. Dennis' personality duplicated many attributes of his father's personality from his speech and mannerisms to how he treated his spouse. He was rude and obnoxious toward his wife, and he knew it.

But love of alcohol was an obvious carry-over from his father.

Scientists don't yet have all the answers on this genetic puzzle. There are many theories attesting to gene transfer and just as many refuting inheritance of alcoholism. Proof is usually in children of alcoholics who have increased risk of addiction. They supposedly may inherit a low level of response to alcohol. This means they can tolerate larger amounts of alcohol than people whose parents were not alcoholics. Studies showing evolving alcoholism in twins separated at birth further support this theory. But so many factors integrate and contribute to increasing tolerance to alcohol that a purist genetic theory is next to impossible.

So, the bottom line for accepting your own drinking problem is to face the facts you know, not the facts you wish were true.

The facts are:

- alcohol is something you developed and drink on your own. Nobody makes you drink it.
- alcohol is poison to your system and gradually destroys vital organs.
- alcohol blocks your sexual potency no matter how sexy you think you are when drunk.
- alcohol masks healthier ways of socializing or confronting life problems.
- alcohol produces high energy or relaxation not naturally produced any other way.
- alcohol interferes with the happiness in people you live with.

Interferes? That seems stupid. If drinking is *my problem, why are others affected by it?*

Good question.

Drinking stifles your own emotional and physical growth but it is like a cancer that spreads infection to other parts of your life. Married drinkers spread this cancer systemically to their spouses and children. Onlookers of your drinking are not inoculated to your habits. They may be accustomed to your drinking and give the impression of accepting it. But don't be fooled. Illusions are tricky. What you see on the surface is never what lies underneath the surface.

Families suffer multiple heartache from alcoholic members. Just so you know, here are the major problems each spouse or child expenses one time or another while living with your drinking habits:

They feel:

Stupid, unloved and rejected.
Angry, resentful, and revengeful.
Scared, apprehensive, and distrustful.
Self-doubtful, desperate for affection, and indecisive.
Ugly, fat, and unattractive.

Spouses are a category in themselves. They are hurt by your passion for alcohol and feel you perfer a drink over being with them. Truth is, you do. Think about when you drink and where you drink. Jerry, for example, spent three nights a week in golf and bowling leagues and went out with his buddies afterwards for a nightcap. He'd return home by midnight and spend marginal time with his spouse. Worse yet, she was pregnant at the time.

Misty drank during the day when her husband was at work. She'd high-tail to local bars and party with other stay-home moms, while their toddlers played in another room or were glued to cartoons. By late afternoon she was wasted and in no shape to communicate with her husband who had returned from work.

While spouses are adults and reveal their needs conspicuously, needs of children may get lost in the shuffle. You may instinctively assume your child is wrapped up in school, playtime or engulfed in their own social world and oblivious to your drinking habits.

Well, you're wrong. Think again. What you don't know is your deadliest mistake. What you don't see is your child watching what you do. Children have impressionable eyes absorbing details of your life like a powerful vacuum. They sweep up every inch of your behavior pattern from your speech and gestures to your daily routines. Emotionally they are your clones. They eat what you eat. They watch on TV what you watch on TV. They drink what you drink.

Ten year old Sammy, for example, lived with his alcohol-drinking mother for 2 years after her divorce. His biological father rarely came around and so his entire exposure to family life was with his mom and her frequent live-in boyfriends. Sure enough, Sammy was the consummate good-son, obediently responsive to his mother's needs. Sammy would get a beer out of the refrigerator for his mother at the precise moment she started her morning binge. When mom finished one beer, trusty Sammy swooped it off of the table and replaced it with another one. He won affection and respect from his drinking mother who absolutely assumed her son was ideal.

Six years later, into his teens, Sammy was not so ideal. He

11

began taking sips of alcohol in his mother's absence and found the taste desirable. He got interested in partying and hung out with an off-the-beat crowd who also drank. In High School, Sammy not only drank on weekends but also began smoking marijuana. He found it fun to hold a joint, smoke a joint, and roll a joint. The secrecy of illegally smoking made his habit more exciting. Now he and his drug-using friends spent many of their days skipping school and smoking joints. When he felt enough buzzes from the joint and slightly tired, he drank two beers for instant energy. The combination of cannabis and alcohol chemically rebooted him so he could function before returning home after school.

Sammy, the ideally obedient son, was in training. He consumed acres of visual images of seeing his mother regularly drink, get high, and be nonchalant about her addiction. Playing into his mother's alcoholism, Sammy felt warmly accepted, loved, and naturalized around alcohol and figured his life was normal by doing what his mother did. As a teen, Sammy's childhood impressions turned from observer to doer; he now put to test the many hours of direct study of his family through channels of peer groups. Sammy never questioned the obvious: Am I chemically dependent? He never doubted his polydrug habits since they followed a continuum of normal life patterns observed during his childhood and adolescence

For Sammy, drug use was like going to the bathroom. You just do it because *that's the way it is. You don't question the obvious and make a stink over it.*

Pride has a new Face

You may have a history of habits like Sammy--or possibly you started drinking for other reasons. Drifter, or Calibrator, drinking began as you discovered alcohol and realized its potential benefits outweighed any hangups you might later suffer. Now you wonder if those hangups you ignored have come back to haunt you. Should you pay attention to the after-effects of drinking such as hurting your family, influencing your children, or disrupting your work day or weekends?

I think so. But here's some good news. Change is not an *all or nothing thing.* You don't have to purge your entire life just to begin a new life. You're not Joan of Arc. You're not General Custer at the Alimo raising up your sword in one last commando strike. Change is never a self-sacrifice aimed at gouging you of everything you know is stable. It's never black or white. Think, instead, of red, blue and yellow. Change is an act of variation. You vary what you are doing just as taking an alternate route to reach a destination by car. If you see a detour sign, you follow the path around the road obstacles until you reach your goal.

Real habit change follows this philosophy. You alter the route you take to achieve a certain feeling, but you use another source of pleasure and not alcohol as the means to your ends.

To become a nondrinker, change gradually takes the following steps and you can perfect these steps by knowing ahead of time what you'll be doing. Here are the steps you can expect to take:

> *Step 1:* *You'll see why you're drinking is too much and is a bad effect on others.*
>
> *Step 2:* *You'll see why habits linger and how you can stop cravings.*
>
> *Step 3:* *You'll see normal ways to be a nondrinker.*
>
> *Step 4:* *You'll discover why even your good intentions get derailed.*
>
> *Step 5:* *You'll see how to keep the nondrinker in you happy.*

Just do, Don't Say You'll Do

The tricky part of committing interest to nondrinking is honesty. You may feel in your heart a real compassion to be a different person. Others acknowledge your efforts as well. They pat you on the back, give you cheerful smiles, and even proclaim support for your objectives. Everybody is optimistic. No Armageddon here. You don't have to face apocalypse to turn your life around and command respect through sobriety. Outwardly the fan club is behind you 100% and is patiently awaiting your first proof of sober-times.

With this cheerleading squad in tact, you may feel strong enough to sell yourself on the idea of not drinking. Internally you've had mental debates over drinking versus not drinking and may temporarily have resigned from this debate by saying, "Hey, if others think I can do it, I can do it."

And, sure, that may be true.

But don't rely on it.

Change is not for what others think of you. You may want their opinions or deeply treasure their feelings about you. That's good. Sensitivity to what people think is helpful. Caring is principally a good stepping stone to self-caring. You want to take a good look at yourself and what you've become. If you really feel life is okay in spite of complaints by your family and friends, then put this book away and drop the whole idea of sobriety. There's no reason to lie to yourself just to please other people.

If you don't want to lie, read on.

Caring goes two ways. Deeply worrying about your spouse, children or family means you deeply worry about yourself. You don't want to wind up with major liver or heart problems; you don't want to be sucking through an IV tube and harnessed in a wheelchair. Nor do you look forward to early Alzheimer's Disease from irreversible neural damage. Forget these medical complications when all it takes is a real commitment to motivate yourself with the same energy you feel to drink. Can you forge ahead being the same person without a beer, wine, or mixed drink? If you're intrigued by this proposition and sure you don't want to end up a cripple, read on. Say to yourself, "Yes, I'm not afraid to be a nondrinker. All I have to do is try."

Chapter 2

Why Bad Habits Linger

Glue. It's probably one of the twentieth century's most incredible inventions. You can stick any two substances together forming an adhesive bond and the objects remain affixed for days on end. Glue is really magnificent. So are habits. And, like glue, habits indelibly stick to your personality for a lifetime unless you deliberately unstick them. Separating habits is a whopper of a job for many reasons and this chapter won't kid you on how easy the task is. It's not easy.

But habit-elimination is possible. People do it all the time with or without professional help. With professional help, you can rely on a trained helper guiding you meticulously through the difficult transition of withdrawals and development of new skills. Caring helpers advise, sympathize and sing your praises every step along the muddied way. Done solo--without a helper--and you may be working overtime to build self-discipline. You're the guardian of your own progress. The metamorphosis through withdrawal syndrome and shaping of new skills is entirely self-driven. Nobody except family may be cheering you on.

Can you do it? Are you ready for the challenge? Sure you are. You can do anything with or without a helping provider as long as you know what roadblocks are predictable along the way. Your roadmap is full of ravines and mountains located in visible sight as you approach them. You can learn where these obstacles are and be preventive. Or, you can ignore the obstacles until later and improvise when you're faced with them. Personally, I'd choose to be familiar with the terrain now and not be surprised later.

Feels Right

Habits linger for three reasons. First, you are not aware you have the habit. Second, habits are noticeable either by yourself or others and you feel complaisant because the habits feels normal. Third, habits are functional. They provide you a means to an end; like Calibrators or Distracters, drinking serves an explicit purpose enabling you to be or act a certain way and enjoy yourself when you are that way.

You're not aware of the habit. Stop for a moment and ask yourself when was the last time you combed your hair. An hour ago? Earlier this morning before going to work? You wouldn't think twice about hair-grooming since it is automatic. You do it without much conscious thought. Many habits are second-natured. For example, wiping your mouth of saliva or scratching an itch on your arm; reflex-like responses blend into your routines without giving them an extra thought. That's what makes behavior a habit. Habits, really, are when some good or bad behavior recurs and becomes intertwined with other routine behaviors.

Drinking alcohol also fits this picture. Think about when you drink beer, wine or mixed drinks. Is there anything else you do routinely when you also drink alcohol? Sure there is. Consider Brad. He is a home-drinker. He finishes his machine repair job by 3:30 PM and gets home by 4:00 PM, an hour before his wife arrives. His regimen is robotic. Brad puts the mail on the table, whips out a Budweiser Light, grabs some crackers, and begins flipping through his mail while gulping down his first Bud. Ten minutes later he grabs another Bud-Light, and gulps that one down, too, still keeping his mind on the mail. Brad is not paying attention to his drinking. His focus is on the mail.

Cheryl gets just as inundated with her kids. After her husband rushes off to work, she awakes sixth grader Jessica and second grader Becky for school. A nudge or two usually does the trick. She heads downstairs into the kitchen and no sooner does she throw a couple of bagels in the microwave when she flips open a Schlitz. She nurses this can with baby-sips as she hurries up and down the stairs keeping her kids on schedule. By the time her kids catch the bus, Cheryl's Schlitz is nearly empty and she's opening the refrigerator for a refill. Two hours later and busily housecleaning, she's "downed" four beers without batting an eye. Asked how much she's drank, and Cheryl would stare at you dumbfounded saying, "I don't know...but look how much I got done this morning."

Brad and Cheryl are not the exceptions; they are the rule. Drinking inherently blends into the routine life patterns so you cannot discern good from bad drinking or detect any drinking at all. In retrospect, you may later count your beers consumed and say, "Geez oh Petes, look what the hell I drank!" But few of us are accountants. You don't keep a running tab when drinking seems as regular as the sunrise. On a cloudy overcast day you may look up at the sky and say, "where is that sun?" Then, and only then are you cognizant of odd interruptions in routines.

That is precisely how habits get interrupted. When normal sequences of life stop suddenly and you're not sure why they stop, you take greater interest in the interruption. Drinking habits interrupt in the same way. But first you have to know your routine like Brad and Cheryl's routines. This is done by isolating the time period you drink and looking real carefully at what you do during that period. Here is a quick guideline to get you started:

Drinking period #1. Here are the things I do when I drink from 5 PM to 9 PM

1. I turn on the TV and sit in the chair.
2. I ask the kids and spouse to say away from me. I say it's my "down time."
3. I surf the channels continuously and end up watching CNN Headline News.
4. I go the kitchen and get some munches--cookies or ice cream.
5. I tune out everything going on in the house. I'm in my own world.

17

This chronology of events charts your common practices during drinking. It's not etched in stone and may vary depending on the weekday or weekend, or if you have company over. Still, you can reliably say it' a fair record of your recurrent drinking habits at night. With this record, choose one simple step in the routine you can stop doing. No, it doesn't have to be drinking. Say, for example, you delete going to the kitchen. Rather than nibble on food, you deliberately stay in your chair from 5 PM to 9 PM without any kitchen interludes. Nor, incidentally, should you cheat and ask your spouse or kids to bring food in from the kitchen for you.

Lacking food, you may discover a sharper self-awareness to routines and increasing attention is paid to how many beers you drink. Now you can do what seemed impossible before. Count the number of beers you drink. One, two, maybe three beers over were consumed over this time period? You're in charge of the record; you tally the score.

Habits are noticeable but normal. Sensitivity to routine is the first mission in habit-elimination. You can lay out the sequence, pattern, and methodically gauge your drinking just by an exercise in self-awareness. Enhancing awareness, however, is futile unless you are aware of something else. That your routines are not normal. Are they "abnormal?" Few people openly admit they have abnormal habits. Even the word, "abnormal" conjures up cruel images of psychotics in insane asylums. And, surely you are not insane. Abnormality also suggests your drinking habits are alien to friends and relatives whose own drinking patterns somehow deviate from your own.

So, you take a mental poll to verify if your habits are so peculiar. Let's see. . .Aunt Jessica drinks from sunrise to sundown, consuming in the neighborhood of twenty beers a day; your dad, you figure, drinks on the average of 10 beers in the course of 5 hours while tinkering with his antique cars. And, your wife, she's a guzzler of 10 beers easily after she finishes her route at the post office and gets dinner ready.

Now that you've compared your notes, you feel reassured your habits are in keeping with family tradition. Good job. You've concluded that everybody drinks the same amount.

I have news for you. All of you are sick.

Routines for every family member you selected all include drinking. They engage in these habits currently or formed the habits for many years. No doubt about it, you are a creature of the same normal habits as your family and feel that what's good for them is good for you. Why change a pattern handed down from generation to generation when it's not really hurting anyone, right?

Wrong. And it does hurt many people; including yourself. Drinking routines regarded as normal are the most difficult ones to break. You have to overcome two barriers before actually abstaining from the liquor itself. These two barriers consist of:

Barrier 1: You have to accept that youre new routines will feel abnormal.

Barrier 2: You have to accept that abandoning old routines does not abandon you.

In other words, don't panic. Realize there is a good and bad outcome of habit changes. The upshot is this: You get a new routine without alcohol and get to preserve your personality so none of you vanishes when you change your routines. The downside is this: Alternate routines you begin doing never feel normal. They feel artificial, forced, and lopsided. You may even lapse into a temporary depression when trying new routines since they are unusual and not perfectly controllable like what you're used to. The worst part are all of the unknowns. For example, if I don't drink while mowing the lawn, how do I know I'll feel good? What if I don't? What if I get bored and want a distraction?

These are all good questions. Answers to them may come in time but not at first when you risk changes in your drinking routines.

Habits serve a purpose. The problem with dangling unanswered questions is this: What happens if I need alcohol to get me through the routine? Without an answer or proof you can make it through the routine without drinking, you'll have no confidence in abstinence. Habits and especially drinking habits may functionally produce an outcome you rely upon. Take mowing the lawn, for example. Harold drinks two or three beers while steering the riding mower and it replenishes his energy after a hard work-day. The ethanol is absorbed by the stomach, enters the bloodstream, and circulates throughout his body, sending neural signals to remain alert. Alcohol guarantees Harold will get the lawn done.

Other purposes served by alcohol-habits may be in social situations. Melissa knows her partner is eager for affection and even with years of therapy still can't get into the huggy-kissy mood. But she's tired of feeling guilty and honestly feels sorry for her partner. So, she compromises: She lowers her inhibitions and induces a strong sexual desire for her partner with two or three beers. Down the hatchet it goes, and she discovers a phenomenal new self emerging who is physically aerobic in bed, deeply passionate, and orgasmic. Sex entirely depends on ingesting alcohol for inoculation against apathy. She performs marvelously when not overcome by distracting negative emotions.

Don't kid yourself; alcohol may get you where you want to go; but you got there on your own. Alcohol was only the catalyst you accidentally installed in your life to guarantee safe passage from not feeling something to feeling something. Just as you drew alcohol in, so you can take alcohol out. The fight for alcohol-free habits that produce outcomes is not easy to win. For most recovering alcoholics in Alcoholics Anonymous (AA) or other support groups, they still haven't really broke these pesky compound habits. Sure, they may not drink; and let them earn a silver or gold coin marking their years of sobriety.

But inspect their lives closely and you wouldn't be so eager to award them a pin or coin. Sober alcoholics may excessively drink coffee, smoke cigarettes, or be food bingers. They cut out alcohol but replace it with God-awful substitutes so they can still get from A to Z using some substance. They may be sober, but they are psychologically still addicts.

For example, now Harold eats Fritos and drinks a ton of sugar ice-tea when he mows the lawn. And you can bet he cuts through that pasture like a bat out of Hell. As for Melissa, her high dose of Tylenol with codeine mixes with over-the-counter sleep medicine. Between both drugs, she attains a soft-silky mood, and feels mentally aboard a fantasy cruise. She is so mellow, so passively permissive with her partner, that sex flows smoothly from her behavior.

Is this what you want? Do you want to replace alcohol with another drug? Can you justify abstinence by adding some new catalyst in your drinking habits? I don't think so. Habit-elimination takes more forceful effort. You really can interrupt drinking as an "operating mechanism" by bulldozing through two barriers. Here is what the barriers are:

Barrier 1: When I don't drink, I won't be able to do things as well as I'm used to.

Barrier 2: When I don't drink, I may feel afraid, depressed, and need help.

Barrier 2 is probably the keystone of anxiety. You may want to drink when you're suddenly unable to perform tasks and require the assistance of another person. Say, for instance, you now feel this avalanche of fatigue previously disguised by alcohol. It's paralyzing. You cannot mow the entire lawn without taking a break or asking your spouse to do part of the lawn for you. When you drank, you prided yourself on being self-sufficient and having the stamina of a bull. Well, sorry bull; you've been whipped.

No amount of will-power can overcome glaring deficits such as fatigue or stress when drinking stops. What can overcome deficits is sheer determination to change your habits and recognize these barriers are not catastrophic.

Others Say It's Right

Habits formed over your lifetime encounter resistance on another level. It's called "popularity contest." By now, for instance, you see how habits feel normal by comparison to family members who also have these habits. You also can see how drinking habits legitimately serve many purposes and can become a stationary part of your life Adding to this normaly is when friends, spouses, partner, and other people you respect downplay changes in your drinking habits. They assert that your drinking is moderate and that "scientists show some alcohol is good for the heart." Well, bully for them.

Drinking in moderation may unclog arteries or even decompose fatty tissues for marginal weight loss, but I wouldn't go quoting scientific research to justify drinking habits. Still, proof is often gleaned from inherently trusting people's advice. Amanda's stepmother Hilda is a good example. She raised Amanda after Amanda's real mom died and her father remarried. Hilda was super in building confidence and guiding Amanda's college-bound career leading to her profession as an attorney.

Now Amanda admires and owes a debt of love to her stepmother Hilda for being inspirational. Hilda also is partial when it comes to overlooking Amanda's faults. When not in court, Amanda gets heavy into the sauce. She drinks two whisky-sours a day and sips from two glasses of wine a night. But her darling Amanda can do no wrong. Hilda is so thrilled with Amanda's profitable legal practice that she dismisses her stepdaughter's alcohol dependence. Amanda has no reason to doubt herself and is blessed with praise from her adoring stepmother. Hilda, like Amanda views alcohol habits as run-of-the-mill in the face of her busy-paced career and mounting success. Since, especially, Amanda's eardrum is attuned to her stepmother's warm words, anything positive that Hilda says will be credible and chiseled in granite in Amanda's thoughts.,

Amanda is not unlike many drinkers caught in the trap of credible testimonials. She was lured by her stepmother's unconditional approval and neither would question herself nor her stepmother, despite fairly obvious warning signs of alcohol disintegrating Amanda's life. The power of respecting authority such as a parent may be hard to break, and you may really feel it's impossible to be abstinent when others think you're drinking is safe.

But don't deflate your efforts so quickly. You've run up against obstacles, that's all. Obstacles are just that; they are temporary obstructions in the path of your goals. One solution, for starters, is to know the barriers you are up against. Here are the three barriers to consider when faced with drinking sympathizers:

Barrier 1: When you break a drinking habit, you feel defiant against a loved one.
Barrier 2: When you break a drinking habit, you may lose approval.
Barrier 3: When you break a drinking habit, you may be told you betrayed a trust.

Betrayal digs painfully below the surface of your skin and pinches a sensitive artery. Nobody wants to be accused of undermining a confidence or appearing deceptive. Just the same, habits you know are wrong and which you want to change may go against the advice of caretakers. These caretakers are less concerned with *what's best for you as they are with averting your sadness or conflict with themselves.* Be wise to loving voices who enchant you with praise when you know in your heart there is a problem and it cannot be ignored.

Scared to Change

Drastically changing drinking habits is a phobia in itself. Who in their right mind would want to undertake this challenge? With all the things that can go wrong, all the unknowns, untoward effects, and disappointments, why do it? Are you crazy?

No. But you're crazier for sustaining dangerous habits that destroy your life. Your fear of change is perfectly normal and builds a wall of resistance. It blocks out enthusiasm for nondrinking and contaminates your thoughts with terrifying visions of hating a sober life, missing the thrill of intoxication, and resenting the passage of wantonness years. Fear decimates your inertia for self-recovery because you persuasively compel yourself to hate anything else but how you feel today; *I don't want to be anything else than who I am today.*

You're trying to protect your self from vanishing into dust.

Because, without that image of who you are and what you do, you'll be lost in space without a clue on how to get back to the vessel.

Are you curious on what keeps you floating up there in orbit without a weight belt? That would certainly solve one mystery, wouldn't it? Well, let's begin by exploring how fear is a defensive mechanism. You unintentionally install safety nets in your life to protect yourself from feeling out of control. Drinking or not drinking, you may spin a web of so many defenses protecting your fragile, vulnerable self, that you don't know which defense mechanism is helping and which is hurting.

I'll point out the hurtful ones.

Ask yourself if these needs are very important to you and occur at least once a day:

1. I need to masturbate or have sex.
2. I need to drink coffee in the morning and many cups during the day.
3. I need to smoke cigarettes.
4. I need to eat sugar in fatty foods such as candy, doughnuts, cakes and other pastries.
5. I need to drink water, soda pop, lemonade, ice tea or some refreshing drink all day long.
6. I need to exercise furiously every day.
7. I need to solicit attention and approval from people every day.
8. I need to buy new clothing frequently or routinely change what I'm wearing.
9. I need to race in my car and get impatient driving behind slow motorists.
10. I need to get angry, explode in a temper or be aggressive at least once a day.
11. I need to feel aroused by watching sports, hunting, working on projects, or feel constantly busy.
12. I need to take many naps a day even though I suffer no physical problems

A "YES" to these needs means one thing. You actively supply many ways to maintain the same effect you get from drinking. Should your drinking stop, metabolic tolerance to Ethanol may diminish and your alcohol may eventually be flushed from your bloodstream. But psychologically the body is still programmed to expect certain sensations generated from alcohol that you now provide through these needs. Take an obvious substitute: sugar. The most addictive ingredient in alcohol absorbed into your liver and destructive to your system is *sugar*. Did you know that?

Sugar is the deadly arrow piercing your organs with its decompositional effects and ruthless aftershock of lowering or raising your glucose causing onset of diabetes. Who wants that? Still, heavy sugar eaters are medical risk takers. Excessively ingesting sweets of all sorts sustains the body's high tolerance for alcohol even when you don't drink alcohol. When you miss a day or two of sweets, expect your body to punish you by feeling extreme cravings and undergoing withdrawal symptoms. That's when you feel the irresistible urge to buy a candy bar at the gas station or drink more soda pop than usual.

Just as sweets keep your body's tolerance at status quo, so do nonsweets Suppose you need to get frantic, angry or blow up at least once a day. Angry people may blame their temper on family heritage--"I have Irish blood in me!" Or you may say your stressful lifestyle constantly puts you in a pressure cooker waiting to explode. Whatever your reason, consider what anger release really does.

It elevates your blood pressure, causes muscular contractions, glandular secretions, and stimulates momentary arousal. Biochemically you are on red alert with all body senses acutely in battle-station position ready for your command to attack. Arousal from anger may be another guaranteed way of assuring your body stays stimulated at a hightened and does not fall below a certain threshold where you feel depressed, sad, and helpless. Alcohol may achieve the same uplifting effect. But when you can't drink, angry outbursts are your backup plan.

Water is the same way. While drinking water is not calorically unhealthy or really equivalent to drinking alcohol, the

amount you consume is identical to overconsumption of alcohol.
That's why they call it "polydipsia." Polydipsia is a pathology
caused by drinking so much water that you oversatiate your
system and feel emotionally afraid to stop drinking water. The
psychological dependency emerging from heavy intake of water
is similar to the psychological dependency on alcohol. Sure, the
liquid is different. So is coffee. So is lemonade. So is Ice Tea.
But excessive consumption of any of these liquids sustains your
body's programmed expectation to be fed high volumes of
alcohol.

That is why recovering alcoholics have high rates of
recidivism. They fall off the wagon many times. They may have
sincere intentions for rehabilitation and prominently earned
months or years of sobriety. But the incipient troublemaker in
their sober process are substitutes for alcohol. Sweets, excessive
intake of liquids, and even angry outbursts represent potential
excitations to the body that duplicate what alcohol does for them.
And that's for people who use alcohol for energy.

The depressant effects of alcohol can be replaced in just as
many ways. Check the list of needs again. How about sleep? Do
you do it a lot? Is sleep an escape from the hustle and bustle of
your day? Like sleep, any excessive mechanisms you employ in
your life to sterilize anxiety is psychologically equivalent to
drinking alcohol.

So, in being a nondrinker, you're really saying *I am willing
to give up all of the substitutes I use to be a drinker.*

Stupid is What Stupid Feels

Change is uncomfortable. There is no way around it. Your
biggest hangup in being a nondrinker probably is not the absence
of alcohol. That's the easy part. The hard part is convincing
yourself that you can endure social humiliation and feel
incredibly stupid due to four reasons. See if you can identify
with each reason:

Reasons for feeling stupid:

Reason 1: I can't believe I drank and ignored everybody else. Now that I don't drink and see what I ignored, I feel ashamed, and utterly stupid.

Reason 2: I can tell my loved ones don't trust me. I feel stupid for being distrusted and not having people rely on me. That shoots my credibility and really defeats any dignity I feel.

Reason 3: I feel stupid for lying. I hate liars. I'd say one thing and do another thing. Now, nobody will believe me and they ignore what I say.

Reason 4: I feel really ansy and out of place not drinking. It's like somebody removed my limbs. I suddenly can't walk, talk, and think the way I used to. I feel incompetent, and know that everybody must see how stupid I look.

You're right, they do. You are one sorry-looking person, with all the makings of a broken down Christmas Tree. You're probably clumsy, confused, and will likely commit more mistakes as you stumble through the rocky road of sobriety. But, hey, is that a crisis?

I don't think so. You're forgetting something. Change is for you, not for others. Recovery may in time be a family affair but for now you are the only one who has to bear the awful exposure of your flaws. Rather than disguise them with defense mechanisms, be open about what you cannot do and learn who you are.

I "Gotta" Do It

Do you get inspired by highway billboard signs? Do those Latter-Day Saints heart-jerking commercials make you cry? Well, don't think you're a Hallmark junkie; you can feel tears, sadness, and even slip into periods of depression as long as you rebound with motivation to be a nondrinker. Part of you already has made this commitment., You want to do it. Emotionally you feel prepared for a new life and can picture days and months ahead of you filled with nondrinking adventures. You will be a renewed person living a renewed life but with the same personality and same body.

Is that all the magic you can expect? Or is there more? Incentives play a big role in selling this new emotional real estate. I'll bet you're half ready to leap into nondrinking and half tempted to call it quits. So, what's holding you back? Still not absolutely sold on the value of nondrinking?

I wouldn't be. Not yet. Remember, nondrinking means you delete from your life all active interest in alcohol or alcohol-related activities including many substitutes we just reviewed which support alcoholic dependency. To do this, and really do this well, you may need a graphically vivid picture of the benefits you can expect from a nondrinking lifestyle. For starters, go ahead and fill in the blanks for each of these questions:

I really want to feel _____ when I'm not drinking.
I really want people to_____me when I'm not drinking.
I really know in my heart I can _____when I'm not drinking.

Now, let's compare how right you are. Take your answers and see how they compute with the following list of rewards as a nondrinker:

As a nondrinker, I can realistically expect that:

1. My family, friends, and relatives will spend more time with me.
2. My drinking friends will respect what I did and will not abandon me.
3. My work or household chores will get done faster and more efficiently.
4. My social life will feature the real me in the starring role and not some understudy who needs alcohol to feel in character.
5. My motivation will increase for career advances and earning more money.
6. My patience, flexibility, and ability to care will be

28

stronger.

7. I will feel genuine love like I've never felt it before.
8. I will not need fake highs to feel confident or superior.
9. I will let my hair down and show my inner self to people who want to know me.

Exposure of you as fully human, vulnerable person is awaiting your first steps into sobriety. Nondrinking is like walking through a dark tunnel where there is light at the end but you can't reach it until you keep walking. You have to trust the darkness and not get frightened.

Then What Happens?

How many miracles do you want? One, two, maybe three? One miracle is medical stability of your body before it deteriorates into a rotting mucous. Another miracle is return of your loved ones through discovery of the caring they have for you and passion you have for them. Still a third miracle is awakening every day knowing you have control. Real control. The type of control that says, "I don't want to do something. bad to myself." Self-discipline is amplified in stereo and is capable of propelling you into unlimited potentials whether in the job market or your personal life.

These outcomes are not as powerfully electrifying as the euphoria you currently achieve from alcohol. Nor do they give you rapid-relief like alcohol did. . Outcomes of nondrinking are not immediate. *They are progressive. They occur over time and grow in intensity as you experience them.*

In so many words, does that mean life will never be as fun as it used to be?

Yes.

But that also means you were not living life. You were living a dreamstate deluded by false hopes, fake needs, and detached from reality where life is never always fun and never always orgasmic. It only becomes fun and orgasmic when you know what you're doing and can regulate your temptations.

Chapter 3

Defuse the Habits NOW

Welcome aboard nondrinking flight 101. On this direct, nonstop flight you can expect minor turbulence and unusual sights looking out your window at an altitude of 3,000 feet. Below the ground may look unfamiliar and you may suffer slight discomfort, fear, and nausea. But rest assured, these symptoms pass. We only ask that you remain seated with your safety buckle on and trust the pilots to get you to your desired destination. We regret that we cannot book you on alternate flights or delay your flight until a more convenient time. Your comfort is our first priority and you must believe that you will feel relaxed by the time we land.

Ready? Let's go.

Five-step Way to Say "No"

Refusing alcohol is a delicate trick you may never know exactly how to master. You've seen anti-drug commercials and even slept through Nancy Reagan's national campaign of "SAY NO TO DRUGS," but never took this advice too seriously. Why should you?

They weren't talking to me, were they?

But now alcohol refusal is an important part of your life. It requires a practical strategy to understand what it entails. So, let's begin with realizing that nondrinking really does not mean saying "NO" to alcohol. When you say "NO" to alcohol, you are still aware of alcohol cravings and begrudgingly lying to yourself outwardly while internally starving for a sip of liquor. Polite refusals at parties or around friends still flirts with your memory of active drinking. You want to eliminate these highly seductive situations and lower your risk of relapse. That's why

31

you can follow five steps to become a nondrinker. These include:

Step 1: *Stay away from places and people associated with drinking.*

Step 2: *Participate in activities or events not associated with drinking.*

Step 3: *Don't talk about drinkers or if you must, talk disparaging about drinkers.*

Step 4: *Increase compassion, helping others, and volunteerism.*

Step 5: *Identify plans and goals advancing your life and career.*

Step 1. Stay away from places and people associated with drinking. Social instincts may draw you to familiar places and around longtime friends with whom you built self-identity. These friends currently may be in high school with you or have been known since high school or early employment years. They laugh with you, cheer you on during your darkest hour, and basically, have shared many experiences shaping your life. They are people you regard as dearly intimate and hope to associate with for years ahead.

Just as they are treasured as friends, so the places you go with them earn a special place in your heart. You can't reasonably abandon either these friends or your club-house locations in the snap of a finger just because you turn nondrinker. Friends are friends for life, aren't they? Yes. They are. Disbanding your inner social circle is not only inadvisable but may cause rapid isolation and make you feel like an unloved orphan. Suddenly nobody would be there to turn to as if you vanished or died. Ending these relationships clearly may backfire, so how can you keep your drinking buddies and not mix with them?

Easy. Invite them to your house. Your house is like *home plate.* Wherever you go, figure it's like batting from home plate and running the bases. Your goal is always to get back to home plate. Go to first base, second base or third base, but always return to home plate. Home plate is safe. It is your sanctuary in

32

which nondrinking rules govern your behavior. That means ask your drinking friends to visit you at your safe place. Inform them not to bring alcohol or simply do not have alcohol waiting for them in your refrigerator. After repeat visits and seeing you're a lousy host by not offering them beer, you're friends may get the message: *Visit me but don't drink around me.*

Where you have more control is over places you go. People's homes, restaurants, retreats, convention centers, night clubs, bars--among other drinking establishments you frequent-- are now off-limits. View them, not as *something you once had in the past.* Rather, view them as nonexistent. *You never had them since they didn't exist.* Entirely dismiss their meager value in your life. To do this, say "STOP" to yourself every time you watch a commercial or listen to others describing these places. The "STOP" follows with "Those are awful places to be in." Automatically, in other words, mentally cast these places into despicable categories of unthinkable, unimaginable places you would ever be in. In a graveyard, for example. Would you regularly visit tombstones in a graveyard unless you were at a funeral? No, of course not. You wouldn't give that place a second thought. It's out of your mind immediately before you start feeling the eebie geebies.

So, instantly your mind disqualifies this location as a place to be. Now you're mind will do the same for all drinking places. Disqualify thoughts and memories of places you historically were fond of to drink alcohol. Do it like this:

Thought	Action
Bar	Dismiss as unimportant.
Jack's house	Dismiss as unimportant.
Red Cedar Grill	Dismiss as unimportant
Bar tent in Westphalia	Dismiss as unimportant

You've expunged these options out of your mind since they are irrelevant to the new way you think. The new way you think is this: I only want places where I've never drank before or that do not have liquor licenses. Describe these places in conversations when you are asked about restaurants or places to go. Unless the topic explicitly is about food or nightlife, do not bring the topic up on your own. Overtalking about social places in spite of your sobriety or their nonalcohol setting will still sound like you're a drinker. It's the old pattern of behavior you had before becoming a nondrinker.

When invited to go to drinking places, think as a nondrinker. Nondrinkers view the world through nondrinking eyes. They never would consider a bar or bar-like restaurant because it's ambiance is undesirable. That ambiance consists of

    a.   loud people talking.
    b.   odor of alcohol.
    c.   dimmed lighting or darkness.
    d.   inappropriate for family.
    e.   potential for violence or promiscuity in patrons

Nondrinkers intuitively erase in their mind any place bearing these features. You can now do the same thing.

Step 2. Participate in activities or events not associated with drinking. By selectively weeding out drinking situations and trying to be open-minded to nondrinking places, you may run into a problem.

Hell, I don't know any clean places to go to.

That's true. You may not. Without your familiar water hole, you may feel insulated from fun and totally miserable. Brainstorming doesn't seem to generate new options and what few alternatives you identify score low in your opinion. *Dennys? Oh God, please, not that!*

You can spin your wheels creating worse options or make life easier by asking three important questions:

    a.   Where do I never go or wouldn't be caught dead going to?
    b.   Where does my family or loved ones want me to go but I never have?
    c.   Where am I so bored that I can't possibly hide my yawns?

I'll tell you where--Church. That's right. Church, synagogue, temple, Kingdom Hall, or wherever your house of worship exists is where you might be visiting. Re-activating your faith is not necessarily the goal here. Attendance and involvement in your religion is the goal. Chances are, your parents raised you in some religious orientation. Catholic, Jewish, Protestant, Lutheran, Methodist, Baptist, or variation of Christianity. Roots of faith trace somewhere in your family history and can be resurrected as part of your new social outings. You can contact your house of worship and get involved either on Saturday or Sunday services or extracurricular programs ranging from Bible Study to Youth Groups to fund raisers. Whether you rejoin your belief system or keep it inactive while participating is entirely up to you.

Other places and activities meeting this requirement of being miserably mundane and pathetic may be *school, your kids' school or extracurricular events,* and *community events.* For teens and high schoolers, get involved in your school's afterschool events. Drama, debate, sports, French and Spanish Club, Key Club--all of these will intrigue you and establish friendships with nondrinking, nondrug using peers. For unmarried adults without children, check into activities at YMCAs and other community centers and clubs, or volunteer at nonprofit organizations once a week or on the weekend. And, for married or unmarried parents with children, the solution for involvement is in the palm of your hands: *Get involved in your kids life.*

Go with them on weekend boyscout, girlscout outings; help them raise money through door-to-door sales, be a classroom volunteer or offer your expertise with afterschool activities. Numerous opportunities exist to indulge yourself in your children's life and adopt their social events as your own. Reclassifying your life as *family-oriented* does not mean you are losing selfhood. Your identity doesn't disappear. You're still there in the flesh and blood. But now you have genuine excitement benefiting you and others who are important to you. You're no longer hiding in your own selfish playground.

Step 3.   Don't talk about drinkers or if you must, talk disparaging about drinkers. Drinkers are entitled to drink. That is their prerogative. But you are a nondrinker and have little sympathy for self-destructive people. You've been there, seen it, and really don't need to watch the reruns. When discussions arise about friends who drink, change the subject or offer negative remarks about their drinking. Yes, that's right. You are intentionally criticizing previous drinking buddies for their uncontrollable habits in contrast to your nondrinking habits. Criticism can be swift and painless and not on a soapbox. Don't glorify yourself with a politically vain speech about your trials and tribulations and how your Skid-Row drinking bums will wind up in hell. Keep the evangelism out of it.

Pride in your nondrinking may hold an advantage for you and may even inflate your ego of feeling superior. Maybe you deserve that superiority. But never forget that even nondrinkers are humble. So, be humble. Be critical, but be humble.

Step 4.   Increase compassion, helping others, and volunteerism. Revisions in your life take many dimensions. Among the greatest for nondrinkers is their unconditional compassion to help others. As a drinker, compassion may have been unthinkable. You probably felt empathy, and possibly cared for a loved one, but repressed those feelings by drinking. Now you can be uninhibited without alcohol by opening your heart and sharing vulnerable emotions with other people. Caring for others means two things. Can you do these?
Caring means:

*I can feel for another person and share with them my feeling.
I can help another person and let myself be their caretaker.*

Deeply abiding love for another person means blocking your own selfish interests and opening up the channels of communication where they speak and you listen. Believe me, that's very different for you. You're not used to doing that. Usually it's the other way around. You talk and they listen. Well, now it's in reverse. Listen with your ears and be prepared to reply with "feeling words." Ask yourself what the person is going through as they talk. Is she sad? Is he happy? What emotions do they display? For example:

The person says	*You then say*
I had a bad day today	Are you feeling really sad?
Our son got an award.	That's great!
My boss was angry.	I'll bet that annoyed you.

Temptation is very strong to do what you've done for many years. You jump ahead past the emotion and try solving the problem. Troubleshooting seems the right approach. You'd hope the person *knew you cared by how you solved their problems*. Wrong. And remember that this is wrong. Troubleshooters are a dime a dozen. Nobody wants one. Tuck it inside and only focus on sharing feelings.

The other side of this coin in offering to help somebody without expecting anything in return except "thank you." Nondrinkers do this. Oh, sure, there are nondrinkers who don't do this and in fact are seriously immoral in their behavior. But largely speaking, nondrinkers are self-disciplined and gain esteem either by their own initiatives or by helping another person. Acts of benevolence accelerate thoughtful and caring traits and kindle a spirit in you of being appreciated for simple things. You can be helpful in many ways and for many organizations. Here is a brief list of people and places who are patiently waiting for your gentle touch.

1. Your partner
2. Your children
3. Your parents
4. Your in-laws
5. Your grandparents
6. Your relatives or extended family
7. Your close nondrinking friends
8. Your place of worship.
9. Your local parks or municipal services (police, fire, ambulance, etc.)

10. Agencies serving disabled or elderly populations.
11. Agencies serving homeless or domestic assaulted spouses

The list abounds ad infinitum and can be searched many times until you find a compatible selection. Outreach efforts to be a helper drags you away from the insulated household, away from drinking, and puts in you contact with a nondrinking people who do nondrinking behaviors.

Step 5. Identify plans and goals advancing your life and career. The final step to initially embark on the nonalcohol enterprise is making more out of your life. Up until now, you probably were tolerant of a low-paying job or repetitive routines, or figured that in so many years you can retire. For 60 plus year olds reading this book, retirement is a valid thought. But I have a sneaky hunch you are a long way from your golden years of retirement and can still generate a spark or two from that rusty thing called your brain.

It takes guts and gusto. Guts is what you have when you take a risk and really contemplate redirection in your career. Can you work another job? How about part-time while caring for the children? If you're a student, how about getting off the merry-go-round and doing your homework? And for college students on the 7-year plan, try something new: Graduate. Be different from who you are. Skills you have are laying dormant in a mental trunk as you grow older. You can let the dust collect on that attic trunk or re-open he trunk and see what you've re-animated.

When Alyce did that she went berserk. She didn't drink but she was with alcoholics. Physically abused, worn down, obese, and self-despising, Alyce had two failed marriages and figured her life was destined to be a punching bag in an alcoholic's gym. She had no idea what suitcase of talents lied underneath her worthless life and didn't even think of looking for that suitcase until one day. That one day when he broke loose out of her defective marriage and moved out of her sewage community into a sparkling new community where nobody knew her and she could be herself. Alyce blossomed using her own pollen and her own ambition as fertilizer.

Today Alyce is a headliner comedianne starring in many metropolitan comedy shows. Her one life-preserver rescuing her from emotionally drowning was faith in her talents. She wanted to start anew knowing the odds were stacked against her. And she did it.

And you can do it too. *You can break out of the mold cast by a bland alcoholic life. You can dynamically blaze new frontiers with hidden talents you know have market value.*

Three-Steps for Others to Help You Say "No

Nonalcoholic enthusiasts are your fan club. They roar at the mention of anti-drink slogans and proselytize beliefs of rigid morality. Mothers Against Drunk Drivers (MADD), National Council of Alcoholism (NCA), and CoDependence Anonymous, AL-ANON, ALa-TEEN, among other grassroots support groups, all share a deep respect for recovering drinkers. Supporters advocate sobriety as the fountainhead for self-cleansing and understood that stages of progress are tedious, frustrating, and counter-intuitive. Should you attend AA meetings or any of its affiliate meetings, expect your courage lifted from this unanimous team of honest helpers.

They are your confidantes, and proponents for change. But team spirit from support groups represents only a fraction of your homebase. Around family, friends and at work you may encounter reluctant sympathizers; people who genuinely are happy for your welfare but who object to bullish nondrinking. They prefer the leisure approach of drinking when you feel like it as long as it is under control. And, remember? You tried that route. It didn't work. So it's not going to work this time around. You've jumped off that bandwagon and joined a wagon with stronger wheels underneath it. Yet, your friends and many family members may not understand why you made the switch.

Do you need to explain? Does Uncle Joe, a lush since age 13, really need a sermon from you on the righteousness of sobriety? Please, no; spare him of that grief. And spare most people rationalizations on why you elected nonalcoholism over alcoholism. The only priest deserving this confession is yourself; remind yourself as often as you want until it becomes memorized by heart. Disclose it only to a selected few people in whom you implicitly trust it will remain a secret.

The trouble with Uncle Joe and the rest of the gang is not their differing attitude but lack of appreciating *where you come from.* In their eyes, alcohol is perfectly normal and is the totem pole around which the family circle revolves. Why a family member wants to deviate from this family circle is beyond their comprehension. You're strange in their eyes. That's what makes justifying yourself so tempting. You feel it in your gut. You want to enumerate the facts on why drinking is wrong and why benefits of nonalcoholism are great. Searching for the correct language to convey your self-revelation may take hours and still fall on their deaf ears.

Don't you get it? They don't care. If they did care, then they'd have to be self-reflective. They would have to look in the mirror at themselves and be ashamed at what they saw. They don't want to do that so they ignore your changes and regard their abnormality as normality.

Knowing you can't effectively persuade stubborn people to think what they don't want to think, try another approach. You can get them to align with your nonalcoholism using two steps. The first step is by jubilantly complimenting yourself aloud and soliciting their praise for your efforts. Second, you can seek their "expert" opinions on places to go and people to see that are nonalcoholic. Now, let's take a closer look at each approach.

Complimenting yourself. Conversations arise for many reasons. You can start the conversation or interject an opinion in an existing conversation. Whichever way you wish, describe yourself positively by describing an recent nonalcoholic activity you accomplished. You don't need to say "it was a nonalcoholic activity," as much as explaining the fun you had with it. Regarding coaching your son's soccer team, for example, say "I had a ball seeing those 4 year olds eagerly trying to kick the ball and falling half the time. They were real troopers."

No matter how cynical or unflattering their replies are, continue as if you didn't hear their stupid answers."Yah, but did you pick up any cute mothers watching the game?" Add more features about the soccer experience including your personal feelings. "I can't tell you how good I felt watching Bobby play like a big guy." After a while smart-alicky remarks fade out and listeners either shift to descent comments or they change the topic.

Treat them as experts. There is more than on way to skin a cat. Treat uncaring listeners as experts. Ask them point blank where they recommend you go for dinner that doesn't serve alcohol or is good for the family. When they return with a wisecrack about a topless bar, repeat your question sincerely and wait patiently for their answers. Ironically, people who disapprove of your nonalcoholism are flattered by your respectful questions and may shift tempo from being ruckus and bowery to informative. As they put on their "consultant" caps and talk in better English, you'll discover these former alcohol playmates who speak in vulgarities can be civil once you selectively pay attention to their appropriate speech.

Whoops—No Substitute Habits

Earlier I mentioned the danger of replacing alcohol with sweets, sex, water, and other foods or activities. Substitutes only delayed physical and psychological change since you keep your body programming in tact and cravings continue on schedule. Real change, you recall, and loyalty to nonalcoholism, meant forfeiting any person, place or object possibly stimulating memories of irresponsible alcoholism. Once it's out of site and out of mind, you can concentrate on solidifying the nonalcohol viewpoint.

That's the first line of attack. A second line of attack is not relying on one particular person or thing as the bedrock for nonalcoholic recovery. You my be an aspiring nonalcoholic and hold tightly onto the rope of your parents or partner for emotional strength. You expect this life partner to have untiring compassion for you and unconditionally to overlook your past scores of mood swings, biting remarks, and drunken episodes where you irresponsibly ignored their feelings. You've given this individual immortality by believing they are a higher order of human beings and capable of forgiveness. And, you may be right. After all, so far your parents or partner loyally are behind you 100% and respond to most of your basic needs.

Does this mean you can take them for granted? Should you assume they will always be there and always adore you like an idol?

NO, I wouldn't. That special person in your life currently is your lifeline assuring you can kick the habit and adjust normally without setbacks. He or she is wired into your mental circuitry with radar vision that can detect your thoughts, slips, and malcontent behaviors way before you act on them. Caregivers are invaluable as guides and can direct your positive efforts when you let them. But, when you put all of the weight of your progress on their shoulders and assume they will carry it, you've made a tragic mistake. You've falsely assumed your loving sponsor will withstand the same torture during your recovery that he or she endured during your alcoholism; that they are gluttons for pain and punishment and only live for your sanctification..

Well guess what. You're wrong. Dead wrong. Die-hard caretakers do have a high tolerance for frustration. They can stomach many more emotional aches than you can and probably have a backbone more stable than your vertebrae. Give them credit for incredible fortitude. Still, they wear down over time when their feelings go ignored and their needs remain overlooked. And when they peter out, they are out for good.

Many cases are known of caretaking spouses who invested tons of time and energy into rehabilitation of their drinking spouses. But after six months of being treated like a slave, they threw in the towel, saying they'd had enough abuse for a lifetime. They pushed way beyond the "quitting point" hoping their spouse would wise up to this abuse and negligence. They even dropped subtle and obvious hints alerting the spouse to change behavior and recognize the caretaker's dying energy. But, no, the clues failed. Recovering spouses were blind. And in the end, these one-time powerhouses of enthusiasm left their nonalcoholic spouses for a better life where they didn't need to work as hard.

Do you want that to happen to you? It will--believe me, it will. Your only safeguard against losing your trusting caregiver is to appreciate what he or she is doing for you and never assume they do it out of duty. *They never do anything out of duty. They do it out of love. Abuse that love and you'll lose it. Recognize that love and give it back with more love and compassion than was given to you, and you'll keep it.*

Good Things to Do Instead

You don't have to be a rocket scientists to ingeniously invent new patterns for a nonalcoholic lifestyle. Social activities you select following the guidelines above of being nonalcoholic are powerful guarantees of relapse prevention. You can almost vaccinate yourself against backsliding when these activities are in place and routinely scheduled. But that means altering an underlying problems you're probably had since you were born: being organized and consistent. How can you do those two things. Already you do some good things. The good things you do such as going to the zoo with the family, taking your partner on a picnic, or spending two hours with your 90 year old grandmother in the nursing home, all are vital to growth when you do them correctly. Do them incorrectly and you'll grow tired of being saintly and wish you'd kept a fifth of vodka hidden in the backseat of your car.

Benevolence is not enough. You have to do good or nonalcoholic things *in a timely and routine manner.* This requires practice of two important skills in organizing your time. First is *consistency.* Second is *structure.*

Consistency means this: You do what you say; and you say what you do. Never promise what you can't follow through on; or if you do, alert the person that you can't follow through before it's too late. Consistency begins when you promise to do a favor or task for somebody. That's nice. Good boy. Now comes the test of delivering on your promise. Promises you make cannot be complex or wishy-washy; they must be concrete and direct. Here's what a good promise is:

> One that is
> * simple and easy to do within the day.
> * needed by the person you're promising it to.
> * achievable without requiring other people to help you.

Promise the world and you'll never get out of your garage. That's why you make your promises in tiny packages that are fulfilled that day. People who see promises fulfilled are not just happy, they are ecstatic. And from their happiness is formed three impressions of you. These impressions directly blast the old alcoholic image and invite the new nonalcoholic image. These impressions are: *First, you are reliable. Second, you can be trusted. Third, you care.*

Can you believe it? All three reactions are predictable from your responsible actions. They earn you rave reviews and a chance at the Gold medal. But for this prestigious honor, follow-through is only a prequalifier. You must show your trusting and reliable abilities extend to organizer daily routines. This is accomplished by setting up priorities and a logical sequence of scheduled activities you can manage. Share this list with your partner ahead of time for his or her input and as further proof of your ambition for structure. Then, with their input, lay out a reasonable blueprint of tasks to do that day along the lines of:

Saturday's List

Time	Things to do	Proof of task done
9:00 AM	Wake up /prepare breakfast	Wife say thank-you
10:00 AM	Go to Sears for new tires	buy tires.
noon	Pick up kids at sleep over	said hi to kids' m mother

1-3:00PM	Dig eight holes for shrubs	shrubs put in
4- 6:00 PM	Watch TV with kids	eat snack
7- 10:00 PM	Take wife to dinner	she thanked me

Planning the day with a fairly organized format does not mean a military regimen of accounting for every minute you are awake. There is plenty of downtime and shifts in schedule due to last minute variations in people's lives, none of which should detour your efforts if you are flexible. Setting time slots is only so that you confine yourself to a definite promise that you and your family can identify and look forward to. As the schedule undergoes change and finally settles with some routine, you build a system into your own and other people's lives that they respond to with their own priorities. Now everybody has an idea of what you do and when you will do it.

The best part of systematic routines is this: No matter how much you hate schedules, managing your time proves you are depending on purely yourself and not another person to make your nonalcoholic recovery a success. The is a self-regulatory effort. It begins with you and ends with you. Nobody is forcing you to do anything except yourself. And the payoff?

It's great. You'll be admired as a pillar of strength in your family and rapidly forgiven for any past mistakes you made.

Chapter 4

Tempted to Give Up?

I'm tired of being a goodie-goodie. No whimpy, syrupy style in me. I see who I was and don't want to change it. So, leave me alone!

Okay-it's a deal. I'll leave you alone. Your family will leave you alone. Your employer will leave you alone. In fact, why don't you hitchhike a ride on the next space shuttle to vanish entirely from sight. Then, nobody will bother you. You'll be left alone without a misery in the world--at least not this world.

Wouldn't that be nice? A stress-free life where nobody makes you do anything you don't want to do. Decisions are on your own. Good decision or bad decision--it's entirely up to you and affects only your welfare. And, sure, in a utopia isolated from civilization and responsibility, unlimited autonomy may be a perfect survival tool. But here in the wicked forest of society surrounded by nosy people and loving families, selfish independence is not a survival tool. It is a menace.

When you don't want to become a nonalcoholic, you're spitting at the people who have worked vigorously to get you there. You're laughing at their efforts, teasing their sincerity, and undermining their integrity. Some joke. Remember, they have a life to live as well. Spending all of their valuable waking hours devoted to your cause is not their cup of tea. Your just one among many priorities squished into their busy day. And, to think you're unappreciative of this loyalty means you may be insensitive to anything these people ever have done for you. So, take a breath or two before getting so upset and really ask who you are mad at.

Is it the caregiver eagerly sponsoring your recovery? Or, are you lodging complaints against the one person who has been most intolerant to your drinking binges--yes, you know who. Yourself.

In this chapter you face the pivotal moment in joining the

ranks of nondrinkers. You ask yourself if life changes are within your psyche and whether leaving a drinking past behind in the garbage is so awful. You alone are the mainframe computing these answers as you fight off old habits and awkwardly stumble through new habits. Navigating through hew habits is not an easy chore. Nobody wants the job and surely not yourself. But you've done it so far and proclaimed minor victories along the way. Going the extra miles until you reach the finish line probably is not any more difficult.

What do you say? Should you stay with the program a bit longer? I dare you to. Read on to prevent getting cold feet at the last minute and wanting to bail out.

It Hurts Too Much

No doubt about it. Transforming from drinker to nondrinker is a painful process. You might as well get it out in the open now, so everybody knows your feelings. Express your deepest resentments, fears, and hostility buried inside your mind. Don't ignore it; freely ventilate it with all doors and windows opened wide and nothing stopping you except air.

The reason quitting hurts is because you go through stages similar to people who are dying. First you pass through a stage of denial in which you try to ignore what is happening to yourself. You believe that if you ignore your problem, somehow supernaturally it will improve and you will be happy again. Next, you become angry as your denial fails and you are forced to face the reality of the situation. You may get angry at things outside yourself such as toward your family, friends, schoolmates and coworkers. You don't really have a beef against them but they are easier targets for hostility than you are.

Next, anger turns to stages of remorse and guilt. It's the stage in which you say things like, "If only I hadn't gotten pulled over by the cops," or "If only my folks didn't smell whisky on me." Re-living faults that brought you to this point weakens your defiance and slowly inches you closer to acceptance of your alcoholism. You even play mental tricks with yourself. Internally you replay scenes in your mind and re-choreograph what you say and do and imagine what might have transpired if these actions replaced the ones you really did. For a fleeting moment you feel relieved and in control. Then, when the mental arcade game ends, reality sets back in, leaving its imprint of unbearable pain.

By the last stage, the one you're probably in now, you're feeling grief. You feel you're losing something very special to you. A trusted companion gone forever. You resist the separation from it and may try viciously to hold onto this security blanket as long as you can until forced to resign from it. As you feel it fade away from you hands, deep sorrow and bereavement overwhelm you. It's like something died, but you don't know what it is.

I'll tell you what it is. What died is a part of you that never should have existed. It's a dysfunctional, unhealthy and ridiculously selfish side of your personality harvested for years without being pruned or destroyed. You can no longer grow this plant inside of you because you've cut off its roots, its water supply, and removed its fertile soil.

It's time to replant another life and patiently wait until it grows. Much of your patience depends on emotional stamina and motivation for self-cure against the multiple obstacles discussed ahead.

Others Want Me to do Bad Things

One disastrous repercussion of being a nonalcoholic and seeing the world through nondrinking eyes is that others may not share your perspective. Last chapter I suggested how you can approach these pesky people and talk their language without appearing righteous or conceited. But dealing with friends and extended family members is one thing. They live outside your intimate bubble and contact with them is minimal. Within your bubble lies the real torture chamber. Your spouse, partner, siblings and parents. These are people, depending on your age, who encircle your life and are inescapable with opinions.

The difficulty with these people is this: they are fickle. On the one hand, congratulate your family. They are strong allies of your cause and hypothetically support your transition to a nondrinking life. Asked if they'd be lifelong helpers, 100% of them would naturally say "Yes" and deeply stand behind their convictions. Still, in testing their words against their actions, another story emerges. Family members may be as hesitant to conform to lifestyle changes as you are and the more you brilliantly shine, the more they fight your improvement.

Are they doing it intentionally? Yes and no. Let me explain.

Family sabotage is really subtle but happens for many reasons. It is when key family players already accustomed to your old behavior patterns developed a lifestyle based on those patterns. This influenced how they think, talk and react. For years, for example, your spouse expected you to return home after 8 PM drunk on your ass. She adjusted to your predictable time schedule by not waiting for you to arrive. She'd plan her activities before and around your drinking schedule and, assuming you'd be out cold by 8:30 PM, she did things without you. At night she'd call her friends, inspect the kids, or preoccupy herself with personal chores totally independent of your life.

Now, with reforming your ways, suddenly life is different. You're not only wide awake and alert at 8:00 PM, but you've been white-eyed and bushy-tailed since 5:00 PM when you came home from work. Well, that's great for you. But, unfortunately, your spouse may have no idea what to do with you or how to change her entrenched habits. Just because you're available does not mean she automatically abandons her schedule and joins you.

The reality of this disjointed schedule is that it makes you feel unwanted.

I don't get it? Here I stop my drinking and do what's right and she's pretending like I'm still drinking? What the Hell is going on here? Will somebody please tell me why I don't deserve her respect?

Oh, settle down. You have plenty of respect. What you don't have is patience.

Just ask Peter. Peter was dating this girl from a broken family who herself suffered enormous emotional hangups. Julie was a drug user, had abortions, and somehow managed to raise a hyperactive kid. Peter believed he could save her but he realized

50

he had to save himself first. He drank 15 to 25 beers a day whether working or unemployed. Peter openly admitted his drinking was abusive and promised abstinence if Julie stopped her drug use. Julie reluctantly agreed and the two finally thought they had a winning relationship ahead of them.

Well, guess what. Another chapter from the Soap Opera began. Two days into Peter's nondrinking career he decided he wanted a Norman Rockwell family portrait in his life and that Julie should greet him with a big juicy smile on her face. Instead, Julie returned home, still sober, with a scowl on her face and a temper fit for a lion. She ignored Peter as she rushed upstairs and hid in their bedroom. The same pattern repeated itself over the next three days. By then, Peter felt his courage of sobriety deserved a medal and Julie should be the one honoring him with it. So, he figured Julie didn't love him anymore and that she was incapable of appreciating his recuperation.

I'll fix her; I'll get even. I'll drink again.

And that's what Peter did. He looped himself around 20 beers that day and felt a pathetic retaliatory satisfaction for hurting Julie.

Trouble is, Peter didn't hurt anyone but himself. He failed to understand that Julie, sober or not, was doing the routine she did everyday. Julie's normal habit was to rush home and hide in the bedroom and take a nap. With her not on drugs, she particularly was tired and desperately needed a nap. Ignoring this reality, Peter presumed Julie was insensitive to his recovery, felt unrewarded by his brave efforts, and decided to restore his old habits.

Julie is like your wife, husband, mother, father, siblings or friends who are wrapped into their own world and simply do not stop the cycle the moment you announce a commitment to recovery. The truth about people is hard to swallow. It reads like this:

Truth 1: Nobody really cares about your recovery. They say they do but they have their own lives to live. Expect them to live them no matter what you do.

Truth 2: People around you don't change as much as you

change. Don't look for changes in them as verification for your own changes. Rely on your own changes as proof of being a nondrinker.

Truth 3: People around you may keep their habits even though you change your habits. Maybe their habits are okay. Don't judge their habits harshly.

Truth 4: Failure for people to notice your improvements does not mean they don't want you to get better. It does not mean they hate you. And it does not mean they are sabotaging your recovery.

Read over these truths very carefully,. Note the part where it says "It does not mean they are sabotaging your recovery." You may object to this statement and really believe your partner or family member is undoing your efforts. You feel you sense their deep resentment and now feel they are getting back at you by spoiling the one good thing you've done in a long time.

You're not paranoid but you are misperceiving the facts. Intimate partners may doubt your recovery and distrust your commitment, but they are not conniving and undermining. *They are not like you are. You might do that to somebody but chances are your loved ones do not.* So, be careful not to confuse your intentions with their intentions. A healthier way to deal directly with hurt feeling of being rejected is to assert the problem in a constructive way. Be prepared for snappy replies they give you and realize these are "roadblocks" to meaningful dialogue. You've caught them off-guard talking about highly vulnerable topics and your family member may not know how to respond. That is why you can equip yourself with a calm feeling-statement that is not defensive. For example:

> *You say:* You're ignoring me.
> *They say:* I'm busy entertain yourself.
> *You say;* That really hurts me

In each case you're opening the doors of your heart and sharing personal feelings in hopes your partner will kindly acknowledge your needs. Sarcasm greets you like a blast of cold air in the face and you may be easily tempted to swear, argue, or give them back a dose of their own medicine. Temptation is fine, but don't do it. Your nondrinking disposition means you stop all urges from overwhelming you; not just drinking urges, but also urges to yell, fight, and protect that insecure inner self you feel has been just whipped. Don't be a three-year-old erupting in a temper tantrum to make your point. Your point won't be made; you'll do the opposite. You'll prove to your significant other how messed up you still are and can't handle life's daily annoyances.

Life Won't Be Fun

Drastic changes in nondrinking are rarely made. You may view the world as a nondrinker; no bars, no food or liquid when you'd usually be drinking alcohol, and no impulses to drop everything and party at night. These instincts are in the past replaced with a moral conscience. And persistent self-control arises when you openly and fully subscribe to six nondrinking rules. These rules help you act and think according to a revised lifestyle faced with brutally unpleasant obstacles, none of which are insurmountable. You can overcome each and every obstacle in your quest for sobriety by understanding the following:

I think before I act.
I ask myself how other people may feel about my action before doing things.
I say no to myself a lot more.
I use prayer or solemn words to reassure my efforts are good.
I rely on me to pull myself through the tough times.
I realize people around me are happy but not ecstatic about my changes.

Adopting these six nondrinking rules is a big part of successful recovery. You may disagree with these rules and even feel they are unfair, such as the one about people not being ecstatic about your changes. But reality is like a shark indiscriminately taking bites out of those who are stupid enough to swim in the shark's den. If you swim in shark territory because you ignored these basic rules, expect to lose a few limbs. Then, too, be a smart swimmer. As in life, use your insight wisely to prevent unnecessary shark attacks by knowing ahead of time what to expect and how to react to the unexpected.

It's Like Going to Mars

Without question, you've embarked on a mission impossible. The more you realize that nondrinking entails a whole new perspective, the more you say to yourself: "I've never done this before and it feels odd." It's like landing on another planet and not knowing your way around. Drinking made life easy. You knew what to do when you felt a certain way. Predictable and routine, your life revolved around a single cause and deviations were few. Instincts pointed you in the right direction and you never missed a beat. Alcohol was your compass guiding you to any destination you wanted.

Now that compass doesn't work. Intuition also doesn't work. Internally the mental navigational system you relied upon for years is defective. Like a plane doing a nose-dive, your panels show arrows going in all crazy directions and you feel you have no clue on how to steer the plane to safety. Heading nowhere, feeling out of control, you're desperately grasping for someone to rescue you. . That is the migraine headache of living in the nondrinking world.

Nobody said it was a picnic. Just as people believe there is a heaven after death--and maybe there is--for others afterlife is not so pretty. It's downright awful. Down 10 feet, to be exact, underground where your body decomposes until there is nothing left but brittle bones. The glorified rosy picture of angels in heavenly clouds helps people cope with dying and unknowns of life beyond death. Supernaturalists personify this picture even more, claiming there are ghosts, poltergeists and other multidimensional creatures who you can become. And, of course, believers in UFOs reassure us there are extraterrestrials regularly abducting Earthlings who promise a better life than what we have.

All of this wishful thinking is to attain immortality. To feel we will never have to suffer horror, death, and awful crises. And, believe me, I really wish these beliefs had enough scientific merit to ease life's painful experiences. But they don't. And changes you make for the better may close the door on one life but open the door on a new life. A life filled with different problems, different headaches, and different solutions.

Nondrinking doesn't spare you the grief of aggravation. It simply affords you a prudent and more capable way of tackling problems before they get out of hand. Fast and efficient confrontation of life's petty problems is your best approach. To do this, plan on a new method of conflict. Historically you may have handled conflict by avoiding the conflict. Now, you face the conflict. Here's how you do it.

Conflict solution #1: Act swiftly to face a problem the moment you experience it.

Conflict solution #2: Stick with the facts of a problem, not your anger. Ask questions and listen to the answers given.

Conflict solution #3: Identify a solution including a compromise; never feel you have to win or be right.

Conflict solution #4: It's okay not to reach a solution except to agree that you disagree.

Family members are so used to you blowing your gasket that they won't know what happened when you are calm. Use the conflict solution steps as general guidelines when faced with tough choices either to be angry or run away. Do neither. Instead, ask questions and stick with the facts in a situation. Oddly, you may discover from patiently listening and sharing your concerns how receptive family members are to your solutions. They always wanted you to be a powerful resource and previously sought your advice to no avail. Now they can count on your counsel as an integral part of their growing lives. That's what makes you a real family member.

Chapter 5

The New You

Nothing is at last sacred but the integrity of your own mind. The eminent author Emerson stated these words warning a generation of people not to conform to the masses just for approval. Be an individual, a self-thinker who relies on your own brain-power to help you through mature decisions. Emerson's insightful words are good advice for the nondrinker. It reminds you of being your own change-agent. Supporters are fine, but ultimately the engine of recovery is fueled from inside you and based on personal goals and objectives.

As you come 180 degrees from drinking and really engage in nondrinking behavior, fears of relapse may diminish and you may be less worried about going backward as you are about going forward. This chapter helps you stay on course with "maintenance" strategies designed to sustain nondrinking thinking and action. With a clear mind and a loyal heart, you can apply these skills for many years without suffering recidivism.

How to Like the New You

What are you afraid of? Failure? Success? Maybe something more specific such as crowded places? Anxiety is a nuisance if you have unresolved fears preventing your venture into the nondrinking life. Recovery, you see, is only half abstinence. The other half is coping directly with conflict, people, situations, and a willingness to undertake risk not prompted by impulse or thrill-seeking. This type of risk is when you apply yourself in high-failure situations while developing new skills. Risk-taking as the platform for self-improvement is the real way to like the new you.

So, how do you get rid of debilitating fears? Let's first consider the range of fears and then strategies to abolish them. Begin by asking yourself if the fear prevents you from regular life routines. Here are some examples but you fill in the rest of your fears underneath my examples:

Fears	What it prevents me from doing
1. Dying	Not much. I can do everything in my day.
2. Driving in snow.	It delays arrival at work.
3. People hate me.	I get intimidated talking.
4.	
5.	
6.	

Fear inhibits action when internally you feel your muscles twitch, body perspire, and stomach growl. No, it's not butterflies. You're suffering a minor panic attack that signals you to slow down and either avoid or escape the situation. *Avoidance and escape are no-no's. Avoidance is when you choose not to do something. Escape is when you're in the fear situation and want out pronto!* By avoiding or escaping, you sabotage your courage by deluding yourself into thinking you can't possibly manage the rising stress and this stress will embarrass you somehow.

Take Laura. She hated the dark. We're not talking overcast here; when the sun went down and lights were off in her townhouse, she freaked out. Laura's terror of darkness traced back to childhood when she was left alone in her dark bedroom by her mean siblings who were playing a game on her. The siblings since apologized, but aftershocks of feeling stifled and suffocated by darkness never got out of Laura's system. Now she'll go to any lengths to assure lights are on in a room.

But Laura also was a drinker. But she made wise choices. She quit her booze and went on the wagon. Her nondrinking ideas were positive; she planned to shift her career from book editor to news journalist and realized it meant digging up stories during daytime and nightime hours. She wasn't a night owl by nature and her fears limited her tolerance to darkness. So, she pulled herself together with a determined goal of eliminating her fear.

First she identified the worse possible scenarios of being in a dark place. She lined up these scenarios from high anxiety to low anxiety and re-evaluated each one for accuracy. *Would I really get that scared in these situations?* Topping her list was hiding in a dark, large storage room waiting for thieves to enter and steal the merchandise. She imagined spying on them in the dark while collecting information for a news story. As she mentally rehearsed this image, she felt anxiety rise up her arm and throughout her chest. She wasn't really in the storage room but the anxiety was as good as real. That prompted her to take two slow and shallow breaths of air and continue to breathe slowly through her mouth.

Anxiety dissipated in seconds while she kept her mental image alive. Now she could picture herself in that musty dark storage room without anxiety creeping in. She was ready for the next step. Laura thought she'd duplicate the storage room to her best ability. While not an exact replica, her living room at night was sizable and got pitch dark inside. So, at 9:00 PM, she crouched down behind her couch and pretended to wait for somebody entering the room. As she waited in the dark, again she felt tingling sensations rush up her arm and knew tension wasn't far behind. Laura immediately did her relaxation routine. She took the breaths, inhaled and exhaled slowly, and let her body calm down.

Good as she was at this, she still didn't know if practice would match real life. So, she asked a manager at large furniture store if he'd mind showing her some samples in the back warehouse. Although it wasn't dark inside and she was with somebody, that didn't matter. Laura walked into the dimly lit warehouse and used the same relaxation steps when she felt anxiety surfacing.

Her methodical efforts may appear cumbersome but they worked like a charm. She found the dark was no longer an enemy. She started leaving her lights off at night and just sitting in the dark doing what she usually did--listening to music or eating. No anxiety occurred.

Just like Laura, nondrinkers faced with disabling fears can remove those fears by following a series of three steps. These fear-reduction steps apply to any fear at all. The steps include:

Step 1: *Construct a series of fear images from bad to worse.*

Step 2: *Picture the worse one in your mind and breathe slowly, calmly and loosen muscles you feel are tense. Do that by tightening the specific muscle area first; then loosen that muscle area.*

Step 3: *Go through each fear image in your mind. Then try it out with real situations resembling the fear images.*

Fear reduction is a valuable tool for public speaking, driving, sharing interpersonal feelings, sex, and knowing how to spend time with people. But be prepared. You may feel childish admitting you have a fear and especially if that fear seems so immature. For example, the fear of talking to your child about his play practice. But don't despair. Nobody cares. It's only you and your own mind that has to know about this fear. And the sooner you do something about it, instead of drinking it away, the faster that fear vanishes forever.

Removal of fears is a steppingstone to saying to yourself, "I am a nondrinker who can deal with the world the way people who don't drink have to deal with it; not by taking any short cuts, but by facing it head-on and proving I'm stronger than the obstacle."

Showcase Your Good Points

Earlier I mentioned the strategy of dealing with unsupportive people by talking about yourself and about your nondrinking. Not as a preacher trying to convert the person, but as proud parent speaking about the accomplishments of his or her child. That is a good beginning for showcasing your good points. Displays of your progress already are obvious by what you do for the family and your routines, structure and follow-through. Such evidence is quite compelling. People really know you are trying and are optimistic about stable recovery. Still, what you do is not enough.

This is because of one reason: *What you say to others is what you say to yourself. Your words of self-praise become your thoughts of self-praise.* Even a hard working nondrinker who is there for every family event and cosmetically appears to be better, may be in denial of his or her progress. You may look okay but say to yourself, "I'll never do it; I can't do this; it's too hard." But, by talking aloud about your virtues, you exercise a moderate amount of vanity without overdoing it. Here is how you can talk about yourself without feeling conceited or too vein. First, focus on what you do right as a nondrinker, not on how you don't drink. Second, always keep it upbeat rather than downplay your progress. For example:

> *Say this:* I had a great time with the kids today.
> *Don't say this:* I didn't want a drink while with the kids.

> *Say this:* I had a lot of energy and felt good.
> *Don't say this:* I can't believe I wasn't tired and bored.

Self-valued comments you make are for two purposes. First is for others to hear it and take note of your inner feelings and acts of progress. That's nice, but not essential. The second and more important reason is this: You hear yourself talk and incorporate your words as valid evidence of nondrinking behavior. That evidence recedes into privacy and internally becomes your context of thoughts. Then, when alone and thinking about your progress, you can reflect using the same positive statements you said aloud earlier. You now think in the language you used to talk to other people.

Be a Leader, Be a Helper

Activities you now do are largely for other people and not yourself. Call it love, altruism, or simply an act of charity. However you describe it, lending a hand to another person is opposite to being insulated and selfish. Years of egocentric drinking blocked out the welfare of others. Now, you've turned your priorities around. You look for ways people can benefit from your expertise and kindness. You lend assistance without expecting goods in return. This is the experience of "unconditional love" I've spoken about throughout this book.

But, like many things initially undertaken as a nondrinker, you may feel charity work has its limitations. You don't want to feel exploited and really hate sacrificing your time purely for another person's arbitrary needs. While such apprehension is normal, is there a way to deepen your appreciation for "unconditional love?" If you think about it, you're perfectly happy to accept unconditional love from another person--in fact you absorb their efforts like an Aardvark. But how about the other way around--giving it back?

Providing unconditional love is not an easy task. Don't think it is. Human beings are inherently selfish creatures and rarely wish to replace personal time for time spent with another person. Even if benefits are obvious being with that person, you still prefer private time over shared time. So, rest assured you are not alone in this struggle. You may never *want to do it, but know you must do it as part of your human responsibility.*

The way to want to help is fourfold. You can get into the spirit of unselfish caring by trying these steps:

Step 1: Ask a person who you love or think you love what you can do for him or her
Step 2: Set a time limit of 1-2 hours of giving of yourself.
Step 3: Ask the person if they enjoy you helping.
Step 4: Tell the person when you are done that you enjoyed helping them

Carefully planned steps of helping take the "I'm a slave" feeling away and give you a sense or moral respect. Outwardly your kindness will be legitimate and persuade the person of your honest remarks. They will regard you as genuinely helpful and in a larger way dispel their stereotyped image of you as an incurable drinker. Unconditional helping does that. Partners, children and other family members all will welcome you into their heart and rediscover your shining qualities. It will be different for them, having spent years tuning you out.

Consider 20 year old Tony. He had hard shoes to follow from the get-go and his drinking didn't help. Two years ago Tony lost his older sister in a fatal car accident after she, herself, rehabilitated her alcoholism. Tony never forgave himself for arguing with her the night his sister drove the car. She was sober; he was drunk. Now Tony faced an uglier situation. His parents were still mourning the loss of their daughter but tried to move on with life. Tony hated seeing them in grief. He hated it so much he blocked out his own bereavement and never visited his sister's grave. His lousy way of coping with both his sister's death and his own problems was to party. He partied big-time.

Initially Tony thought it was funny that he should stop smoking marijuana and be a nondrinker. He felt kids his age deserved to make Friday and Saturday nights party nights and thought his parents knew this. But they didn't. And even if they did, his parents were nondrinking, conservative and religious. They thought Tony was irresponsible and headed for the same fate as his sister.

When Tony decided his drinking was a problem, he meant it half-jokingly. Sure, he recognized alcohol consumed his social life and interfered with school. Sure, he admitted his parents were unhappy with him. And, sure, he confessed to drinking as a way to forget his sister. But Tony also drank to prevent being with his parents. He viewed them as outsiders totally incompatible to his way of life and incapable of understanding him. He really wanted to move out of their house but knew financially he could not do that. So, to "play the game," he conceded to limit his drinking to once a week and do more with his parents.

That was torture to say the least. Tony complained about his parent's awful taste in music, movies, and food. He resented forfeiting his time to be with them *on his weekend.* But Tony kept his promise and stuck it out for another two weeks. That's when he changed his tune. As his drinking reduced from one night to no nights, Tony spent more time with his parents. He ate dinner with them, talked to them about little things and also his feelings, and even went out to the movies with them. He did all of the things he initially hated to do with them. Within a month, Tony suffered a relapse; no, not with alcohol. With guilt.

He lapsed into deep remorse and shame, realizing that he had almost lost his parents the same way he lost his sister. He suddenly exploded with tears over his sister's death and blamed himself fully for her tragic accident. He hated his drinking side and wanted to be closer to his parents, partly to protect himself from drinking, and partly to replace what he had missed from them.

In the end, Tony discovered unconditional love. He did all of these initially detestable activities with his parents and found them not detestable. He came to care; by genuinely giving of himself over his selfish needs, Tony found closeness with his family and the security of knowing his drinking days were over.

Make it Stick

How do you keep sobriety in tact? Sure, you can join the ranks of millions who attend support groups twice, three times and even four times a week. That's fine. You can hear their stories, share your own stories and distill down from these tales important data for your own life. You can also join a religious or other "spiritually" bonding organization such as the Knights of Columbus, Hadassah, or Bible study groups. Active participation can strengthen your insights of yourself and other people, while broadening your commitment to a fraternal group. And third, you can do what most recovering alcoholics do: You can monitor your progress with the declarative word of the Twelve Steps model.

According to this model, you admit you are helpless against the cunning and baffling power of alcohol and require a higher order to guide you through the recovery path. The twelve steps essentially say:

1. Admit you are powerless over alcohol.
2. Believe in a higher power to restore your sanity.
3. Turn your will over to God or some other power.

4. Make a moral inventory of yourself.
5. Admit to yourself and God your wrongdoings.
6. Ask God to remove these defects in your character.
7. Humbly ask God to remove your shortcomings.
8. Make a list of all those people you harmed and make amends to them.
9. Make those amends where possible.
10. Continue to take personal inventory and admit wrongdoing.
11. Seek serenity of self through prayer and meditation.
12. With spiritual awakening, carry your message to other alcoholics.

Stories you've heard of alcoholics turning to the Twelve Steps for salvation largely are true. There are many religious and nonreligious recovering people who swear by the steps and preach this gospel as mandatory for rehabilitation. These survivors say you can identify with the words if you incorporate them into your personal life. Abiding by the twelve steps keeps you sober, respectful of your addiction, and cognizant of the difficult road you face every day. You will hear this basic message from all users of the model from nondrinkers to therapists, and will feel a strong urgency to adopt this model or else you'll be losing out somehow on a panacea. A cure.

But watch out. The twelve steps are not a quick-fix. They are not a guaranteed antidote for years of uncontrolled drinking and ruining your family life. Even elders of the Twelve Step model agree: faith in the model means you have to have faith in yourself and in the skills needed for nondrinking.

So, you can incorporate twelve steps into your daily prayer or personal self-talk. You can move upward the steps as slowly or rapidly as you like and gauge your progress as proof of getting healthier. The twelve step model is not incompatible to the steps introduced in this book. But, nor are the steps alone going to save you. Without the skills specifically outlined on building nonalcoholic behavior and knowing how to handle others, you can kiss your progress good-bye.

The way to make your nondrinking skills stick, and really

stick, then, is to go beyond the twelve step model. You have to use the POWER reminder. POWER is an acronym that stands for *Proof, Ownership, Weakness, Empathy,* and *Risk.* Here is what each of these words mean:

Proof: Proof is clear and convincing evidence of your nondrinking lifestyle either demonstrated by what you directly do or what people say you do. There is no guess work. No theory, no abstraction, no inferences. You either are a nondrinker or you are not a nondrinker.

Ownership: Ownership is the privilege of knowing you do not depend on people for your nondrinking recovery. Others may generously support you, but you remain the principal change-agent who entirely is responsible things you do right and things you do wrong.

Weakness: Weakness is the evidence of being humble, admitting mistakes, and forgiving yourself and others for wrongs . Similar to the *5th step of the Twelve Steps,* this means you volunteer your faults in a nondefensive manner and open your ears to criticism.

Empathy: Empathy is giving unconditional love, support, and unselfish time to family, friends, neighbors and strangers who can benefit from your skills and expertise. Empathy also is your barometer on how *caring you are toward problems in other people. Do you share and talk about their feelings?*

Risk: Risk is the entrepreneurial feelings that you can embark on any task or confront any problem providing you face your fears head on and fight the traps of avoidance and escape. Risks are what motivate you to join organizations, change your career, or get involved with projects or tasks you'd never believe were possible a year ago.

Use the POWER reminders as one uses a Franklin planner. Consult it regularly as a litmus test of your actual progress of improvement. Check it to verify if nondrinking is really a life pattern you've interwoven into your personality. Nondrinking, remember, is not a state of alcohol cessation but a holistic perspective on the world. You look at everything in front of you as a person who never drank. Does that mean you repress your drinking desires? Does that mean you bury your previous life as a drinker?

No to both. You never need to repress what you won't feel. Nondrinkers never feel cravings to drink since they handle impulses with self-discipline and have never depended on any substance--alcohol or other. As for burying your secret past, you can't bury it. The losses or gains you had during drinking days remain part of you today and are the bedrock of your personality. Changes in personality as a nondrinker incorporate who you were then with who you are today. You don't replace the old with the new. You blend them together creating a stronger you, much more capable of fighting life's incessant problems.

But more to the point: As a nondrinker, you do not need to be reminded of your drinking past or how much you no longer drink today. Focus instead on new behaviors you do today that are different from what you used to do. Look at your family, friends, school, employment and thrive on how well you use these resources to better yourself. That is really who you are. A manager of different behaviors producing incredible and delightful changes for everybody around you.

And when you see these changes happen, don't be shy. Speak up. Stand proud. And tell others about your improvement and why you love who you are.

Chapter 6

Hey, Family Members: How not to Sabotage the Sober Person

What do I do? How many times do you say, "I'm not sure how to handle this family problem?" Problems take many forms. Does your spouse drink too much alcohol? Is a family member also emotionally ill? Has a spouse or child been diagnosed terminally ill because of drinking? Answers to these questions put your own recovery in motion.

Ask yourself,

How do I not feel guilty?
Why do I hold feelings inside?
Why do I get anxious a lot?
Why do I get so angry?
What should I do to help myself and my family?

Here's how. You're scared and don't know what to do about it. That is, until you have a direction. This chapter doesn't provide all of the directions, but it supplies a roadmap to begin your recovery journey.

How to Talk, Listen, and Share Intimacy

This is your best step forward to a new life, to a new beginning. Do it gently but do it proudly. Realize that any new beginning is a transition in your life. You're just growing, not going backwards. Nor are you *starting over from where you were before all the problems in your family began.*

The biggest step is breaking the vicious cycle of defective family routines. Do so with your drinking spouse or family member by following these basic exercises:

1. Ask your family member a question. Let he or she

answer it. Don't be thrown by their tone of voice or word choice.

2. Now, repeat their sentence using your own words. But choose one or two of their key words in your re-statement.

3. Repeat their sentence and use emphasis on certain words like they did when they spoke. Don't be a parrot.

4. The whole time you repeat what they're saying, keep your opinion out of it. No defending, apologizing, justifying, or trying to be nice.

5. When you hear their side, tell them what you liked about what they said. Even if you disagree wholeheartedly with their views, that's okay. But first tell them *what you did like about it.*

6. Now, say the following: *I can see where you're coming from, but let me tell you my thoughts on this matter.*

7. Resist proving your point. Just say it once. Resist defending its merit. Just say, *Thanks for listening to me.*

Talking to one person is good. Talking to all family members is harder. Should there be ground rules in family discussion? Yes. Here's the basic ground-rules for getting the conversations off to a positive start:

Ground-Rules for Family Conversations

1. **Nobody** blames another person.
2. **Nobody** is defensive or has to explain "why" they did something.
3. **It's okay** to share a humiliating or embarrassing experience.
4. Tell what you feel and stick with the facts.
5. **Admit** in your opinion that you may be wrong and you want input from the family.
6. Have the family follows steps "#1-7 above."

The next hardest part about talking and listening is *sharing*. Sharing begins by sharing neutral events. Then, share negative events about somebody else; and finally, share negative events about yourself. Encourage your sober family member, other family members or yourself to do the following:

1. **WEEK ONE:** Tell your family neutral (plain, simple mundane) things you did during the day. No big deal on the small things. Offer a play-by-play of the general schedule.

2. **WEEK TWO:** Tell your family negative events about somebody else. Recall bad things happening to a friend, neighbor, relative, or in the newspaper. Stick with facts, no assumptions. Don't entertain too much discussion on why and wherefore. Just stick with the facts.

3. **WEEK THREE:** Tell your family about one or two things you did that were negative. That means sharing things you feel embarrassed or humiliated about. Expect them to laugh at you, even to tease you about it. That doesn't mean they disrespect you or think you're weak. It means they don't have the foggiest idea how to react to your honesty. So, you're seeing them stumble at their worse. Let it happen.

Be positive: Steps everybody goes through in Recovery

You know you go through stages. Predictable stages. Stages that involve accepting, rejecting, and even hating the situation you're in. Here's a brief description of what you or the sober person probably felt going through stages of recovery.

Desperation and Abandonment

Feeling afraid, torn, insecure, out of control, unstable, and desperate to restore normalcy in your life. You feel strong urges to rectify the family at any cost and by making high sacrifices without rationally thinking through choices. Desperation sparks fears of being abandoned, unwanted, hated, and horrible thoughts of being a failure. Ending drinking doesn't seem enough. Impulsively you grasp for straws on solutions to reverse family decay and make things better. When things don't get better--or get worse, you panic.

Anger and Resentment

Anger arises when you can't fix the family or drinking family member. Many obstacles block progress. Alcohol, drugs, another romantic relationships, parents, children, jobs, even culture and religion can stop the headway made. You hate this interruption because it ruins your plan to fix things. Helplessness makes you feel resentful, trapped, besieged, betrayed, and deceived. You blame the drinking person or even children for misleading and manipulating you. Anger projects outward onto all family members and not onto yourself.

Distrust and Isolation

Hating yourself for being tricked, you pull inward. Suspicion replaces trust. Things people say and do are doubted and felt to have ulterior motives. Distrust is not just with others, it is toward your drinking partner and any person or family members. Feeling distrust protects you from being hit broadside again and from making similar mistakes. Distrust lets you hide, stay home at night, and make excuses to avoid and escape social events. Insulating yourself feels good, feels right. The more you take refuge in your safe home, the more you feel problems go away. Trouble is, problems don't go away. They get worse and your interpersonal skills deteriorate.

Relief and Motivation

You expel anger in small and large outbursts. You feel on the rebound. You conclude the family member hit bottom for a good reason. The drinking partner or child did you a favor by sparing you the grief and aggravation of being the rescuer; you hated being the lifeguard and wanted somebody else to clean up the family mess. Anguish turns to relief as you feel vindicated from shame and put behind you the misery of family problems. You feel renewal of energy, optimism, and prospects are stronger to make yourself better and meet people. You turn this bad situation into a door of opportunity. And now you want others to witness your discovery of happiness.

Recovery and Confidence

Recovery stage is literally just that. You feel refreshed, healed, and a different person. You still see "the old you" in the mirror but you feel like a different personality. Less crying, less worrying, less self-blame. Life feels balanced with bad things not upsetting the good things that happen to you. Everything is taken in perspective. Now is when you focus on personal goals and are very cautious about always saying "Yes," or catering to people. Old habits of caretaking are replaced with perceptive, judicious thinking. You use new standards on judging good from bad decisions and can say "No." Confidence results from knowing the new you is consistent, stable, and advancing in the direction you want.

How not to Sabotage Progress

Seeing the family member or yourself recover can be an exhilarating experience. Or, it can be an exhaustive one. It all depends on how well you fight off urges to slip back into the same old family mold. You don't want that mold. You want to break that mold in two and start over. But sometimes you can't break away that easily. So, here's what to do.

1. *When you distrust the progress of the sober person* . . . . . *THEN:*

Step back and admit you don't have all the answers. Write down on a piece of paper how vulnerable you feel and why you're scared. Don't try to regain control by being bossy or mean.

2. *When you resist the progress of the sober person . . . . .*
THEN:

Realize you're fighting your own progress. It feels very strange making changes that you think you don't have to make. But why not make them? You're bound to benefit from it? Just try an experiment. Go along with the changes in spite of your insides telling you it doesn't feel right.

3. *When you want to protect the sober person. . . . . . THEN:*

You're trying too hard to accelerate the progress. You can't do it by taking charge and making it happen faster. Your mouth has tasted hope and success and now you want large spoonfuls of it. Well, sorry. No adult portions allowed, not in recovery. Only babysize portions are acceptable. Just let the sober person go at his or her pace. Let that person stumble. Let that person slightly backslide. Don't worry. Backsliding doesn't mean going backwards. You'll know if that happens and you'll be prepared to stop it away before the family member or you hit bottom.

4. *When you have high expectations for the sober person . . . .*
THEN:

Chop them in half. Go slower. Go easier. Go simpler. Don't expect the person to recover like you would recover. He or she is not you. They are not your clone. You're you; and they're them. Let that person go at his or her own pace and downsize your expectations. Real expectations come from discussions with the sober person on what is and what is not possible to accomplish. No guesses. No fantasies. No delusions. Just goals that are real. Talk it out with the sober person and get a realistic gauge on how he or she is doing.

5. *When you perceive the sober person is ruining the family . . . .*
THEN:

It means somebody--maybe not you--is afraid to change. You're afraid that change will cause *chaos*. That all the rules of the household will go to pot. True, these rules may be defective or dysfunctional. But they are the rules. So, nip it in the bud by looking at recovery differently. Rather than think the sober person is spoiling the family, think of him or her as a newborn. The family has to adjust to the newborn because the newborn is *a joyous addition to the family*. Perceive change as a positive experience opening doors to new experiences.

6. *When you suddenly feel angry and resentful. . . . . . THEN:*

It's simple: Talk it out. Let out the steam. Be up front and direct about your emotions and ideas. Use language that it honest and caring. But stick only to the facts, not assumptions. Don't ventilate your feelings about the last twenty years of being deprived, abused, or deceived. Those years are gone. They are not coming back. Forget them. Those years are history. Forgetting the miserable past doesn't mean you wiped it off the planet; you didn't invalidate your past. All you did is validate the present. Talking about your revival of optimism lets you change in healthy ways. If you must express anger, do so. But combine anger statements with how you're currently handling anger in your life and why you're happy with recovery in the family.

Remember, a positive approach in airing your views always results in constructive conversation. The sober people in your family already know the benefits of constructive conversation and are eager to renew their affections and loyalty with your help.

Chapter 7

Special note to Adult Children of Alcoholics

When you get what you want, in your struggle for self, and the world makes you king for a day, just go to the mirror and look at yourself and see what that man has to say. For it isn't his parents, or preacher or friend, whose judgment upon you must pass. The fellow whose verdict counts most in your life is the one staring back from the glass. Some people may think you're a straight shootin chum, and call you a wonderful guy. But the man in the glass says you're only a bum, if you can't look him straight in the eye. He's the fellow to please--never mind all the rest. For he's with you clear up to the end. Anonymous).

An adult child of alcoholics is not a person. It is an experience. Children raised in households where a father or mother drank heavily witnessed the normalcy of alcoholism and family reactions to it. Sadness, anger, conflict, confusion and shame all comprised the mixed emotions dumped on your impressionable mind. Toddlerhood to adolescence, you saw one or two parents ingest alcohol and a bit of bravery and thought nothing of it. That is, until now.

Now you notice a myriad of funny reactions in your personality. Sure, you may drink-but that's an obvious consequence. What about the subtle influences bled into your life as you grew up. Like, for example, feeling sensitive to what people to say to you. Or, absolutely detesting conflict. Odd, erratic or even superstitious habits such as perfectly lining up coats in the closet to compulsively exercising, all trace to peculiar learning experiences you had around the drinking spouse. This chapter introduces you to key habits you may have alerting you to the Adult Children of Alcoholics (ACOA) syndrome. Once you know you possess these habits, don't despair. It's not like contracting aids. It's not contagious. But left uncured, and like a cancer it can spread ferociously throughout your life, damaging your ambition and relationships.

After you discover if ACOA features fit in your life, the chapter helps with first-step strategies to repair the damage and get started on a new foot. Like the forever sober drinker, ACOA recovery is never instantaneous. Small steps are normal. Pace your growth in efforts you make, not in outcomes you achieve.

Are You an ACOA?

Not surprising, offspring of addicted families have many commonalties. Some commonalties overlap with children raised in nondrinking households. Physically, sexually or emotionally abused children may display quite similar behaviors, even though the abuser never drank. In common, then, is not alcohol per se; but effects drinking has on the parent who acts abusively or inconsistently. Among drinking-reared children, here are the leading signs of adult distress:

Enabling/caretaking

Adults afraid of conflict or of risking behavior changes find they please satisfy other people's needs. You may find you lose yourself by caring deeply about how another person feels. Caring makes you emotionally invisible or unimportant compared to the visible deeds of more needy people you invest in.

Efforts are usually methodical and systematic. You bend over backwards to appease a lover who you believe will want you more after you prove your worth. Failure to prove this worth leaves you feeling guilty, helpless, and terribly rejected. Consequently you rebound with catapulting energy to try again and prove beyond the shadow of the doubt how indispensable you are.

Aggression

ACOA anger takes two forms. First, anger arises when you feel loss of control and to look vulnerable. Second, anticipating conflict, anger flares as a warning to "predators" (negative people) to stay away . Aggressive acts in advance of criticism is a defense mechanism to avoid conflict. You find discordance a phobia and down-right paralyzing. No sooner does somebody get angry at you, when you feel the hair on your neck stand on end and your chest feels tense. Fear anticipates that something bad is around the corner--usually a person who is angry at you.

Anxiety and Panic Disorder

A mad rush of dizziness, loss of breath or rapid breathing, weakness in limbs, tachycardia, ear and eye sensitivity comprise symptoms called *panic attacks*. Panic attacks arise when you literally feel trapped in an anxious situations without a clue of what to do. It reminds you of being cornered by an angry parent about to terrorize you verbally or physically. As an adult, there are no threatening parents around; just your memory of them.

But it feels the same, nonetheless. Impending anger or conflict arouses great fear and mobilizes you to figure a way out of the mess. When you can't find a way out, impending anger turns to impending doom and you feel claustrophobic; fear asphyxiates you into a choking spiral of terror that is only relieved by running away.

No Communication

You simply withdraw and remain mute under any impending threat of conflict. Attempts to penetrate this silence is met with poor eye contact, crying, or additional efforts to seek safety in a hidden spot.

Runaway

You physically run away to another location. Relocation can be at parents' house, friends' house, bar, or driving long distances in unspecified directions.

Substance Abuse

You drink beer, mixed drinks, smoke a joint or other chemical use in anticipation of conflict, rejection or criticism.

Emotional Paralysis

Panic and fright happen simultaneously when you are confronted and feel totally helpless. Lacking alternatives, your only survival instinct is emotional paralysis. You just freeze. You feel numb, and anesthetize your body until the wave of fear passes.

Selective Attention

This is opposite to emotional paralysis. Perceptual abilities became sharper under threats of conflict, criticism or rejection. Astute thought, sensation, and observation alert you to subtle ways to avoid or escape unpleasant situations.

Passivity

You literally play dead. A passive posture neutralizes unwanted predatory attacks. Persons who electively withhold comments wait for the aggression, criticism or rejection to finish; then they resurrect pleasant topics or move the discussion rapidly to safe territory. You appear on the surface as loving, empathic, compassionate and deeply caring. Inside, however, you are jittery and deliberately careful not to venture opinions to anybody less they think you are stupid.

Accusation

Just the opposite of passivity is accusing others of wrongdoing. Accusations primarily arise for two reasons. First, anxious and annoyed, you may have improperly inferred information from the predator or environment. Inferences motivate you to bullishly blame predators for acting irrationally or being nasty to you, even if they really were not the reprehensible. reprehensible.

Feign Ignorance

Passivity, emotional paralysis--all serve to withdraw from perceived conflict. Another avoidance tactic is pretending you simply are ignorant of facts or problems presented in the conflict. Ignorance liberates you from justifying answers, coming up with solutions, or dealing in any way with surface anger. .

Imposterism

This is a very serious ACOA symptom. Fear of looking stupid, or exposing your faults may elevate your sensitivity to people's perceptions of you. Instead of admit what you don't know, you may find you fake knowledge. Faking knowledge or nodding in agreement on things about which you know very little creates the impression of strength, pride and intelligence. However, underneath this charade is your anxiety; you shiver fearfully that other people will *spot your stupidity and discover your are an impostor.*

Shame/Martyrdom

Avoiding anxiety takes another twist. You may feel compelled or obligated to release other people from their burdens. Shame does this. You relieve the predator of anger by blaming yourself for causing some problem. You voluntarily receive punishment and spare another person grief.

Recovery Guidelines

Therapies of all genres are available for ACOAs. Choices vary from classical psychoanalysis to structured behavior therapy. Group therapy options also can be valuable. But no matter which therapy or therapist is helpful, goals should address behavior patterns produced by *punishment* and *deprivation*, especially *avoidance and escape*. Following is a list of goals and strategies recommended for your therapy.

1. *Change beliefs.* Altering irrational beliefs or impure inferences begins with identifying the inaccurate rules governing your behavior. Beliefs most dangerous are self-critical beliefs. Defeat these beliefs by (a) interrupting the beliefs, (b) asking questions of the person from whom inferences are drawn, and (c) replacement of self-criticism with self-complimentary and realistic statements

2. *Basic Assertion + Self-expression.* Basic assertions are questions asked of another person about words or actions possibly misunderstood by observation alone. "Why did you do that?" requires a brief answer that clarifies motives, reasons, and obviates your inference that offensive or uncertain action must *be due to something I did.*

Self-expression further includes three parts. First is *disagreements.* Second is *opinions.* And third is *criticism.* Disagreements commit you to make refusals or directly dissent with opinions expressed by other people. Opinions are spontaneous statements interjected in a discussion.

When practicing these step make sure you do not use *defusal tactics* . Defusal tactics vary depending on individual history but generally take five forms. These include: (a) Apologies, (b) discrediting, disqualifying statements, (c) defensiveness, (d) self-criticism, and (e) compensating.

Apologies . Apologies accept blame for assumed discomfort imposed on the listener and relieves the listener of supposedly acting negatively in retaliation for the discomfort.

Discrediting, disqualifying statements. Perceived discomfort in the listener may trigger you to dismiss, discredit or disqualify opinions you just made by admitting they may be wrong, or that little validity supports the statement, or by deferring judgment to the listener's alleged expertise.

Defensiveness. This is when you mistakenly fight back with *rationalizations* that seemingly justify your actions.

Self-criticism. Attack against yourself instantly is believed to relieve imminent conflict.

Compensating. Feeling ashamed, you might instantly make up or *compensate* for any inconvenience by generously accommodating the listener in some capacity, either by relieving them of responsibilities or providing them with a service or resource guaranteed to win back their friendship.

3. *Reversal of Guilt.* Steps that prevent guilt are twofold. First step is for you to reverse guilt back to the listener, seeking more facts about the matter: "Was I supposed to go to the grocery store?" Fact-finding questions serve the dual purpose of collecting critical objective information rather than relying on inferences. It also puts the onus of responsibility upon the listener's shoulder. A second step is literally to *blame the listener* for mistakes or faults instead of you absorbing the blame.

4. *Resist Rejection.* Steps to follow under rejection include:

1. Delay responding for 3-5 minutes. Resist engaging in defusal tactics.
2. Assertively state what the person said and your emotional disapproval of it.
3. Walk away and ignore subsequent roadblocks, attacking remarks from listeners.
4. Make self-statements that it is okay for people to be upset with you.

5. *Building trust.* Fear can impede progress toward building trust unless you identify your fears and face them. Steps generally involve:

1. Telling personal, embarrassing or humiliating situations to a significant other. Resist using defusal tactics when telling the stories.
2. Ask significant others for favors. Ask them to

do jobs you usually do or believe nobody else can do. Accept the product of their efforts regardless of errors or the inconsistency between their efforts and your own efforts.

3. Ask a significant other to plan, organize or direct social, business events that typically is left up to you.

4. Permit the person to make decisions or initiate efforts you typically handled yourself, without your interference even if the person asks your assistance.

6. Break impostor syndrome. Remove this syndrome in two ways. First desensitize yourself; that is, make verbal statements aloud on how you can handle a nervous situation. Second, once you are in embarrassing situations, *stay there!* Force yourself to survive verbally or nonverbally around people. Look at vulnerability as a challenge not as a disaster.

7. Risk-taking efforts. Take spontaneous risks regarded as foolish, childish, and posing further hazards to vulnerability. First construct a list of social, sexual or playful activities you envy in other people and want to do yourself. Next is to figure out if any of these activities exist in your personality. Try on these new activities or behaviors as if you were trying on a new outfit. Impersonating people you admire may feel fake and almost scary.

But you are auditioning their behaviors in much the same as children imitate other children and parents growing up. When you grew up, opportunities for healthy imitation never existed and you lost valuable experiences. Now, it's catch-up time. You'll find the exercise is invigorating and really builds confidence.

8. Anger control. Control over fear involves control over anger. Changes in self-statements, in muscular tension, in visible cues, and toward altering time pressures represent steps in arresting anger.

9. *Disabling enabling.* End caretaking tendencies using in three steps: (a) resist rescuing, (b) resist pleasing, and (c) demand reciprocity

Resist rescuing. You must refuse temptations to rescue, thereby allowing victims to suffer. This also means resisting suffering *vicariously* the emotional grief and guilt associated with ignoring people. Instead, become detached like a spectator able to walk away without commitment.

Resist pleasing. Don't try this until you can be assertive, overcome roadblocks and express opinions without defusal tactics. Do two things at once. First, withhold pleasing gestures. Second, do selfish things. However, never compensate for selfishness by doing for others because you feel guilty.

Demand reciprocity. Demand an exchange. For every personal sacrifice or concession made there is a dividend earned: You literally ask for something in return. It doesn't matter what it is, *as long as you request something.*

10. *Construction of emotions.* You already know how to get angry and be afraid. But can you feel love, passion and intimacy? If not, you need to follow a threefold process.

First is to trust another person and relinquish control. Second is learning basic touching, from simple hand-holding or extended hand gestures to simple kissing (with a spouse or intimate). Affection in private is broadened to public displays of touching, embracing and even kissing. Physical forms of exchange accompany verbal compliments and self-affirmations of looking and feeling feminine or masculine and looking attractive to a partner.

Touching moves to the next step of sexual intimacy. Arousal first is attempted by self-stimulation and by letting a partner caress erogenous areas around your upper and lower torso. Foreplay that is exciting continues for longer intervals instead of being a boring prelude intercourse. After foreplay is satisfactory, strategies are learned to build up plateaus (for women) and stability of erection (for men).

Finally, show affection around your children or parents.

Tough as it is, you want your offspring to see that affection is normal.

By now, you probably have an idea of what an ACOA is. Signals of disabling ACOA may go beyond the symptoms reviewed here. Worse symptoms can include medical problems or repeated relationship failures. You may also find it necessary to seek individual therapy addressing one or many of these symptoms in a more comprehensive manner. Therapy is a good beginning to clearly understand antecedents to your misadventures and ways to turn your life around. Steps you take affirm not only do you seek sobriety but that your recovery is holistic. *You aspire a complete, well-rounded change encompassing every troublesome habit.* Habit-removal promises a new personality and beats the odds against relapse. That's when you've really become *forever sober.*

About The Author

DOUGLAS H RUBEN PHD is a family and addictions psychologist and media consultant. He is author, co-author and "scriptdoctor" of over 40 books, two screenplays, and over 100 professional articles. Seen on DONAHUE and two national infomericals, plus TV and radio coast to coast, his recent self-help books include BRATBUSTERS: SAY GOODBYE TO TANTRUMS & DISOBEDIENCE; NO MORE GUILT: 10 STEPS TO A SHAME-FREE LIFE; AVOIDANCE SYNDROME; FAMILY RECOVERY; 60 SECONDS TO SUCCESS; and ONE MINUTE SECRETS. He also wrote the blueprint for other authors with YOUR PUBLIC IMAGE: TV, RADIO, and PRINT MEDIA IN CLINICAL PRACTICE, and WRITING FOR MONEY IN MENTAL HEALTH. Remaining books are scholarly for college libraries. Dr. Ruben is in private practice and president of Best Impressions International Inc, a media consulting firm.